AN ELDER'S
PUBLIC PRAYERS

An Elder's
Public Prayers

Toyozo W. Nakarai

SECOND EDITION, REVISED AND ENLARGED

Exposition Press   *Hicksville, New York*

Second Edition, Revised and Enlarged

© 1968, 1979 by Toyozo W. Nakarai

First published, 1968

Library of Congress Catalog Card Number: 78-74642

ISBN 0-682-49351-1

Printed in the United States of America

Contents

Preface to the Second Edition   7

Preface to the First Edition   9

CHURCH   13
    Church   13
    Ministry   14
    Church and Ministry   19
    Ordination   20
    Inauguration of a Minister   21
    Inauguration of Officers   22
    Baptism   22
    Marriage Ceremony   23
    Funeral Service   23
    Memorial Service   25
    Mothers' Day   25
    Sunday School   26
    Guest Speaker   27
    Ministerial Meeting   28
    Missionary Conference   31
    Rural Church Institute   32
    Ground Breaking   33
    Dedication of a New Unit   34
    Dinner   35
WORSHIP   37
    Invocation   37
    Pastoral Prayer   41
    The Lord's Table   61
    Offering   123
    Benediction   126
SCHOOL   131
    School of Religion   131
    Honor Day   140
    Baccalaureate   145
    Commencement   147

Founders' Day 148
Annual Conference 149
Annual Banquet 149
ROTC Commissioning Ceremony 150
Inauguration of a President 151
Inauguration of Faculty 152
Thanksgiving 152
Christmas 153
Easter 153
Benediction 154
MISCELLANEA 157
General 157
Adoration 162
America 162
Bible 163
Christian Growth 163
Christmas 164
The Cross 164
Faith 165
Freedom 167
Human Achievements 167
Humility 168
International Banquet 169
Knowledge 170
Light of Life 171
Man 171
Mission 172
Peace 172
Prayer 173
Race Relations 175
Rededication 175
Sovereign 182
State Legislature 182
Thanksgiving 183
Tree of Life 183
Truth 184
Wisdom 185
APPENDIX 189
An Elder's Private Prayers 189

6

Preface to the Second Edition

A decade has passed since the first edition of this book was published. In three years it was out of print, and since then I have received many inquiries about a second edition. However, due to other obligations, I was unable to put the material together until now. I am grateful for the patience of many friends who have waited so long for the appearance of this edition. Many prayers were added to those of the first edition, some corrections were made, and several samples of my private prayers, to which I referred in the preface of the first edition, are found in the appendix.

Some of my personal friends, including one or two editors, thought that modern English expressions would be preferable to obsolete words and phrases; but the fact is that they are found even in the Revised Standard Version and the New English Version of the Bible for prayers. On the other hand, many other personal friends advised me to keep the prayers as I had written and used them. This latter advice I have accepted. However, I must confess that in my private prayers I do not use any sophisticated or formal words, and I am inconsistent in my choice of words. The prayers are written in conversational English, but occasionally antiquated words and even foreign words appear.

All scriptural quotations are my own translation of Hebrew, Aramaic, or Greek texts of the Bible, even though they may appear identical to those of well-known English versions. Designation of chapters and verses follows that of the traditional English Bible.

Once again I wish to record here the debt I owe to my wife, Frances, who read through with critical eyes the new prayers added to this edition and made several suggestions for improvement. She also reviewed the manuscript when it was completed.

September 5, 1978
Johnson City, Tennessee

TOYOZO W. NAKARAI

Preface to
the First Edition

I have been an elder of a Christian church, an ordained minister, and a professor of the Bible. Of these three appointments, I regard the eldership as the most important, for this responsibility covers every sphere of my life including the ministry and professorship.

As an elder I pray in private and in public. My private prayers are spontaneous, informal, and constant. I pray while driving, and I pray while lying in bed. I pray while giving counsel. My words are unrefined, and my thoughts are not always orderly. I just speak to God, praising Him, thanking Him, confessing to Him, and asking Him to use me, even me, for His cause. Sometimes I ask for His blessings for the people who are in need. Other times I beg Him for health and comfort for the sick and destitute. In all this, I firmly believe that God responds according to His will, if my prayers are right. The short prayer below is a sample of my private prayers. These are the words that I spoke when the news of the Japanese attack on Pearl Harbor reached me on December 7, 1941. (I was born in Japan.) This prayer has been in my mind ever since.

Were I to live tomorrow, I would die for the Christ.
Were I to die tomorrow, I would live for the Christ.

When I am asked to pray in public, and if I am informed of such ahead of time, I do much preparation. I must confess that sometimes this is the cause of agony lasting an entire afternoon and evening, not because the assignment is painful, but because I cannot find the words suitable for the occasion. Other times the thoughts of the expected audience seem to flow into my mind without any effort. In any case, the words that I gather together may be those found in the Bible or other books of a devotional nature, or they may be just those that I use daily. However, for public prayers my expressions are more or less formal. When I complete my first draft, I let my wife look at it, or I read it to her. Then the prayer may be revised according to her reaction. By this time, I have transferred the prayer from the paper to my mind; I never read a prayer in public.

This book contains the public prayers that I have used, though I should state that they were not always uttered word for word, for, moved by the spirit, my expressions may have changed here and there. Just before I pray in public, I always ask God to let me say what He would have me say, and this gives me peace and comfort. At any rate, I acknowledge here the debt I owe to my wife, Frances A. Nakarai, who has been my severe but constructive critic in writing these prayers.

August 7, 1964   Toyozo W. Nakarai
Indianapolis, Indiana

AN ELDER'S
PUBLIC PRAYERS

LIST OF ABBREVIATIONS
FOR THE NAMES OF THE BOOKS OF THE BIBLE

OLD TESTAMENT

Genesis	Gen.	1 Kings	1 Kings
Exodus	Exod.	1 Chronicles	1 Chron.
Leviticus	Lev.	2 Chronicles	2 Chron.
Numbers	Num.	Ezra	Ezra
Deuteronomy	Deut.	Job	Job
Joshua	Josh.	Psalms	Ps. (*pl.* Pss.)
2 Samuel	2 Sam.	Proverbs	Prov. (*pl.* Provs.)
Ecclesiastes	Eccles.	Micah	Mic.
Isaiah	Isa.	Habakkuk	Hab.
Jeremiah	Jer.	Haggai	Hag.
Amos	Amos	Malachi	Mal.

NEW TESTAMENT

Matthew	Matt.	Philippians	Phil.
Mark	Mark	Colossians	Col.
Luke	Luke	1 Thessalonians	1 Thess.
John	John	1 Timothy	1 Tim.
Acts	Acts	2 Timothy	2 Tim.
Romans	Rom.	Hebrews	Heb.
1 Corinthians	1 Cor.	James	James
2 Corinthians	2 Cor.	1 John	1 John
Galatians	Gal.	Jude	Jude
Ephesians	Eph.	Revelation	Rev.

Church

CHURCH

O Thou, breath of life, despite the roar of bombing planes and the boom of battering cannons, the rose of Sharon speaketh Thy law and the lily of the valley uttereth Thy love. Lest mankind forget the ultimate creative authorship in Thee, do we humbly dedicate this service to the Christ. Forbid that we pray for miracles and wonders that Thou mayest bestow upon us, but we do ask for steadfast strength and wholehearted consecration equal to our tasks and duties. May the glory of Lebanon displace human distress. May the excellency of Carmel supplant social disorder. May the cross of Jesus dispel worldly disbelief. In our savior's name we pray. Amen.

NOTE: Written during the Second World War.

* * *

Our heavenly Father, we thank Thee for Thy grace which has brought us together in order that we may enjoy this fellowship. We thank Thee for the old members of this church, to whom we owe our past experience. We thank Thee for the new members of this church, to whom we owe our future growth. Above all, we thank Thee for the young and the old who are now present, to whom we owe this beautiful demonstration of the unity of ransomed souls. Guide us as we march on toward the perfect image of Christ, and bless our ministers as they wholeheartedly serve Thee and Thy people, to the end that Jesus Christ be glorified. In his name we pray. Amen.

MINISTRY

Our heavenly Father, our trust in Thy promise and our faith in Thy son impel us to place our all in Thy hands. We thank Thee for Thy grace that enables us to serve Thee. We thank Thee for Thy command that enables us to serve Thy creation. Be with us as we abide in Thy name. Yea, let us be with Thee as we preach Thy word. Bless those whom Thou wouldst. May those who suffer for Thy sake feel the embrace of Thy tender love. Amen.

SCRIPTURE: Josh. 1:6-9.

NOTE: "Ministry" means service; a minister is a servant. The word "name" in the Bible sometimes signifies person.

* * *

We thank Thee, O Lord, for these holy words that are eternally true. As we stand at the threshold of Thy kingdom, we pray that Thou wilt enable us to be strong and courageous in ferrying Thy people to the promised land. May we not swerve, but may we have confidence in Thee, for Thou art our shield, our refuge, and our redeemer, forever and ever. Amen.

SCRIPTURE: Josh. 1:6-9.

NOTE: Moses, the servant of God, was dead. Joshua, the son of Nun, stood on the eastern bank of the Jordan. There lay before him the promised land. If Palestine were the kingdom of God, we might be compared to Joshua.

* * *

14

Our Father in heaven, we thank Thee for the blessed office of Christian ministry. Realizing our inability and many faults, we bow before Thee once again. Grant us intelligence to declare our faith. Give us courage to follow the Christ. Amid the roar of battling cannons, the command of human idols, and the surge of un-Christian forces all over the world, may we each proclaim: "As for me and my people, we will serve the Christ." In his name we pray. Amen.

SCRIPTURE: Josh. 24:14, 15.

NOTE: Written during the Second World War.

* * *

O God, we thank Thee for the light of Thy love that pierces through darkness, for the cross of Thy son that saves all mankind, and for the sheep of Thy fold that Thou hast entrusted unto us. We do not pray for wealth, nor riches, nor honor, but we do pray for Christian wisdom and knowledge. May it be Thy will that Thy sheep be cared for properly. To the shepherd of shepherds, even the Christ, be glory forever and ever. Amen.

SCRIPTURE: 1 Kings 3:5-14.

NOTE: Upon succeeding his father David, King Solomon made a sacrifice at Gibeon. There, realizing the great responsibility that was to be borne by him, the new king prayed for wisdom and knowledge. "Wisdom and knowledge" in this prayer means wisdom and knowledge of God.

* * *

15

O God, we now enter into Thy glorious presence, and thank Thee for the new covenant that Thou hast given us. And lo! We realize that we are "undone," for we are the possessors of "unclean lips" living among the people of "unclean lips." We shrink, but we are ready, O Lord. Cleanse us of our sins by virtue of our faith in Thy word. We are meek, but we dare, O God. Send us into the most difficult fields, and give us the hardest tasks. Here we are; use us for Thy sake. Amen.

SCRIPTURE: Isa. 6:1-8.

NOTE: King Menahem of Israel sent a bribe to the Assyrian king in order that his kingship might be safe. King Uzziah of Judah died. Syria and Israel were about to invade Judah, but the material wealth of Judah was dulling the religious consciousness of its people. It was then that the call came to Isaiah.

*　*　*

We humbly bow before Thee, O Lord, trying to realize the significance of the highest duties and privileges that are ours. We repent with shame, for we have been blind and staggering servants to Thee. Take complete possession of us as we call upon Thee. Break open the sealed book. May we read therein, not the commandment of man, but the principles of Christian ministry. We ask this in Jesus' name. Amen.

SCRIPTURE: Isa. 29:9-16.

*　*　*

Father, we thank Thee for these precious words, more precious than any words of human counselors. As we meditate upon these thoughts, may our pride vanish, and may we gain that wisdom and that peace. Enable us to dedicate ourselves more fully to the upbuilding of Thy kingdom. Help us to win more souls for Thy sake. In our savior's name we pray. Amen.

SCRIPTURE: Prov. 11:2, 11-14, 30, 31.

*   *   *

O Thou, creator of all, who by Thy supreme intelligence brought forth the universe out of chaos, and who by Thy unexcelled wisdom appointed man to rule over Thy creation, we praise Thy name. Help us to become more conscious of Thy divine call and of our sacred mission. Enable us to hear Thy voice. Dispel the darkness within us, and fill us with the light of the cross. May the cross of Jesus endure forever, world without end. Amen.

SCRIPTURE: Luke 11:1-14.

17

Mission

Eternal God, for Thy creative wisdom and redemptive grace we praise Thy name. From the earthly dust to the living soul, and from the living soul to the everlasting glory, Thou hast paved the way of the truth. Enable us to find the unlimited riches in wholehearted sacrifice. Help us to bear the ancient cross in this bewildered world. Grant, O Lord, sufficient power, steadfast virtue, increasing faith, and saintly intelligence to the lives dedicated to Thy missionary cause. Exalted and magnified be Thy golden throne of the Christ. In his name we pray. Amen.

*   *   *

Our Father in heaven, we thank Thee for the Christian conception of the world, its beauty, its goodness, and its truth. We thank Thee for the Christ, the essence of the harmonious unity of the universe. Enable us to carry on our commission as learners of that teacher, in Goshen, in Nazareth, in Galilee, in Bethlehem, and in all other parts of Thy creation. Strengthen our faith as we bear the cross. In Jesus' name we pray. Amen.

NOTE: "Learners" means disciples.

18

Teaching

Blessed be Thou, O Lord, creator of the universe and Father of mankind. There is none beside Thee. We thank Thee for Thy saving grace enacted by Thy own lamb of Calvary, which has brought us to our teaching ministry. As we now assemble here, let us remember the seriousness of the tasks which Thou hast placed in our hands. Let our thoughts be clean. Let our words be pure. Let Thy heavenly wisdom descend upon Thy servants, and let it enlighten our souls. Let it brighten our course. In our savior's name we pray. Amen.

CHURCH AND MINISTRY

Blessed be Thou, O Lord, Father of mankind. With humble hearts and contrite spirits do we invoke Thy blessings upon this assembly. Though mountains fall and oceans surge, let Thy word be our guiding light. Though flowers fade and leaves fall, let the beauty of Thy holiness sanctify our souls. Though nations war and governments rage, let Thy peace be our rock of refuge. Glory be to Thy ministry. Glory be to the ancient cross. Be with us, O Lord, forever and ever. Amen.

NOTE: God's "peace" means completeness, safety, health, welfare, tranquility, contentment, and friendship.

*   *   *

O Thou, master of creation, we thank Thee for the shepherd of shepherds and the lord of lords, even Jesus Christ. We pray for the church universal and for the ministry ecumenical. May Thy church follow the gleam of Thy light. May Thy ministry magnify the glory of the cross. Let Thy church be as strong and firm as the roar of the lion of Judah. Let Thy ministry be as delicate and tender as the fragrance of the lily of the valley. May the smile of goodness prevail over the taunt of evil. May the power of faith overcome the force of death. O great Spirit, we dedicate ourselves to Thee. Let us walk with Thy son through the sweet communion of the saints. In our savior's name. Amen.

NOTE: "Ecumenical" means universal.

ORDINATION

O Lord, humbly do we join this laborer of Thy harvest in confessing our faith in the sufficiency of the Christ. Grant him the wealth of Thy spirit and jewel of Thy wisdom. May he bear the torch of Thy gospel and the banner of Thy salvation. Like the prophets of Israel let him speak Thy word. Like the apostles of Thy church let him magnify Thy son. Use him according to Thy will, and guard him against human authorities. Let him feel the surge of the power of Christ now and evermore, to whom be glory, world without end. Amen.

NOTE: "Gospel" means good news. It may be understood as God's story.

*   *   *

Mighty God and merciful Father, humbly do we approach Thy throne of grace and thank Thee for the Christ, for his church, and for his good news. We thank Thee especially for our brother John Smith and his wife who have dedicated their all to the cause of our savior. Wilt Thou bless him and his labor in the days to come, but now let him feel the surge of the power of Christ upon him. Henceforth, let him preach with prophetic courage, let him administer with priestly insight, let him counsel with saintly wisdom, and let him shepherd with Christian love. O God, guard him, keep him, teach him, guide him to the end that the ancient cross will be glorified. Though mountains fall and seas rage, let Thy word stand forever and ever. Through Jesus Christ, our lord, we pray. Amen.

INAUGURATION OF A MINISTER

Blessed be Thou, O Lord, king of the universe and Father of mankind. Thou hast ordained the golden path from the finite to infinite, from the sinful to the godly, and from the mortal to the immortal. We praise Thy name. We thank Thee for this congregation of the saints who have nurtured it from its infancy to its manhood. We thank Thee for the consecrated men and women who have brought us our brother in Christ who is to become our leader, our teacher, our prophet, our counselor, and our evangelist. But in the growth of this Thy church and in the call of this Thy minister, let us gratefully sense the working of Thy Holy Spirit. Father, bless him according to the gifts Thou hast bestowed upon him, and bless us as we become co-workers in the ever-widening ministry of the church universal. To this end we humbly invoke Thy blessing upon this assembly. Thou hast blessed us long, O Lord. Lead on, O king eternal. May Thy will be done. May Thy will be done. Through Jesus Christ, our lord. Amen.

INAUGURATION OF OFFICERS

O Lord, we thank Thee for Thy love, so tender and so merciful, that it shields even a bruised reed. We thank Thee for Thy word, so righteous and so true, that it enlightens even this confused world. We thank Thee for these consecrated men and women, so humble and so loyal, that they dedicate even themselves to Thy cause. May Thy guiding spirit rest upon them, as they serve Thee and Thy children. May now and henceforth these officers and the rest of us embrace a renewed faith in the Christ, a faith that withstands even the quaking earth and the surging sea. In our savior's name. Amen.

BAPTISM

For the excellency of Thy handiwork in the heavens above and on earth below, we praise Thy name. We thank Thee for the star over Bethlehem among the luminaries of heaven, and for Thy beloved son among the wonders of earth. May the heavens be opened and the Holy Spirit descend upon those who partake in this initiatory rite of Thy kingdom. And as they march henceforth toward Thy golden throne, may the rod of the shepherd of shepherds protect them, and may his staff sustain them. Through Jesus Christ, our lord, we pray. Amen.

SCRIPTURES: Pss. 19:1; 23:4; Acts 2:38; Rom. 6:3, 4.

MARRIAGE CEREMONY

Blessed be Thou, O God, who from ages past to the ages to come ordained the manner of man and woman to enter the estate of matrimony to multiply themselves, to subdue the earth, and to serve Thee. Be with us as this man and this woman declare before Thee and before these witnesses their cherished faith in each other, dedicating their union to the way of Christ. To him be glory forever and ever. Amen.

SCRIPTURES: Gen. 1:28; 2:24; Matt. 19:5; Mark 10:7, 8.

FUNERAL SERVICE

O Lord, in whose hands rests the destiny of man, even at a time like this, we praise Thy name. We praise Thy name, for Thou art the healer of the wounded. We praise Thy name, for Thou art the comforter of the bereaved. We thank Thee for Thou hast released this precious soul from his earthly struggle, transmitted the abundance of good found in him to his children's children, and hast established thus the living memorial for his sake. But now, O Lord, bless and guide his family and others who knew this beloved soul. Grant them courage, fortitude, and peace, with which they may also share the eternal life. Through Jesus Christ, our lord. Amen.

SCRIPTURES: Job 5:18-27; John 14:1-4; 1 Thess. 4:13-18.

*   *   *

O God, our Lord and our Father, even at a time like this we thank Thee, for Thou hast released this precious soul from her earthly pain and suffering, and placed her in the eternal bliss of Thy care. We thank Thee for her faith in Thee and for the beautiful memories of her which are transmitted through her children and children's children. Let them be a living memorial for her sake. O Lord, bless, comfort, and sustain the members of her family and all others who knew this beloved soul. She has left us for a time, but she lives, she lives, she lives! Amen.

Minister

Praised, exalted, magnified and extolled be Thy name, O God of mercy. Thou hast raised John Smith to be Thy minister. Now Thou hast called him to Thy heavenly realm. We confess our faith victorious which enables us to thank Thee even at a time like this, for his ministry endures forever. As it was to the advantage of his disciples that Jesus passed away, so may it be for the enlightenment of those who knew him that John Smith was taken away. As the snow and storms of the winter foreshadow the flowers and birds of the spring, so may the passing of our beloved minister bespeak the fruitage and harvest of his labors. To this end wilt Thou bless this Thy church, and let our souls declare in the days to come: "He lives, he lives, he lives!" Through Jesus Christ, our lord. Amen.

> NOTE: John 16:7 says in part, ". . . it is for your good that I am going away. . . ."

MEMORIAL SERVICE

We thank Thee, O God, for the Christian faith that pierces through the doubts and fears of human life, and opens for us that vista of eternal life. We thank Thee for the precious lives that have been dedicated at Thy altar for the cause of Christian faith. May our memories of such men and women help us in the growth of our own Christian wisdom and virtues. Help us to be seekers of the truth, O our redeemer and savior. Amen.

SCRIPTURE: Prov. 14:25-34.

MOTHERS' DAY

O Thou, creator of the universe, Thou hast created man in Thy own image and according to Thy likeness. Male and female hast Thou created them. We praise Thy name. As we humbly assemble here on this day and participate in this act of worship, we thank Thee for Thy countless gifts of grace, especially for the Christ and his church. But on this day, let us also honor mothers of mankind, remembering their pains and sorrows, and their love and devotion in bringing up sons and daughters. As we must love the Christ as he loved us, so let us tenderly love our mothers as they lovingly gave us life on earth. Father, may Thy loving care attend our mothers, and bless us all according to Thy will. In Jesus' name we pray. Amen.

SCRIPTURE: Gen. 1:26, 27.

SUNDAY SCHOOL

Biblical Study

Our Father, we thank Thee for the book of books that has been handed down unto us by the sages of the past. Watch over us, as we examine ourselves in the light of Thy word. Guide us as we seek for Thy truth. Speak face to face, as we yield ourselves unto Thee. Let our thoughts, our words, and our acts become acceptable in Thy sight, O our God and our redeemer. Amen.

> NOTE: The Bible is a collection of little books. In fact, "Biblia" does mean little books. It is sometimes called the "book of books" because of its significance. The Jews often identified themselves as "the people of the Book." This has been adopted by Mohammedans and Christians.

Promotion Day

Mighty God, merciful Father, as another cycle of our educational ministry becomes history, we thank Thee for those who faithfully taught, and for others who earnestly learned. We thank Thee, above all, for the Christ, to whose peace we have been called in one body. Enable us to attune our human peace to his cosmic peace, and let it prevail over us, world without end. Through Jesus Christ, our lord. Amen.

SCRIPTURE: Col. 3:12-17.

O God, we thank Thee for our Christian fathers and mothers, our Christian brothers and sisters, and also for all the rest of the members of our Christian families, teachers, and friends, for they have brought us up to be Thy children. We thank Thee for the beauty, the liberty, the justice, the wealth, and the abundance of Christian America, for here we may truly practice Christ's teachings. As we praise his name in music, may we rededicate ourselves to Thee. Help us to become more worthy of the devotions of our families and of the heritage of this nation. As, nursed by nature, trees bud and flowers smile, so, nurtured by the Bible, may we grow into Christ's image and likeness, in whose name we pray. Amen.

GUEST SPEAKER

Blessed be Thou, O Lord, for Thou hast created order out of chaos and paved the way of salvation from a sinner to a saint. Bless our speaker according to Thy will, and enable us to embrace the doctrine of the Christ. In our savior's name we pray. Amen.

NOTE: "Doctrine" means teaching.

MINISTERIAL MEETING

Invocation

We wait for Thee, O Lord, let us rededicate ourselves to Thy cause. We wait for Thee, O Lord, let us behold Thy countenance. We wait for Thee, O Lord, let us hear Thy voice. We wait for Thee, O Lord, let us renew our faith in Thy word. Bless this assembly of Thy ministers according to Thy will. In Jesus' name we pray. Amen.

Ministerial Rededication

Omnipotent God, omnipresent Lord, and omniscient Father, we praise Thy name for the love of Christ brought us together once again to renew our fellowship of the new covenant. But our souls cry within us that we are undone and unclean, so we are unworthy of Thy ministry. Yet, we cannot but declare that we have dedicated ourselves to Thy cause. Wilt Thou cleanse us, re-create us, and reclaim us for the ministry of the Christ. Let the new covenant bind us ever closer unto Thee, and let us thank Thee for the fetters of this divine bondage. We thank Thee, O Lord, for the burden of the cross, which Thou hast graciously placed upon us. In Jesus' name we pray. Amen.

> NOTE: "Omnipotent" means almighty, "omnipresent" indicates being everywhere, and "omniscient" signifies having infinite knowledge. "New covenant" means new agreement. The New Testament contains the new agreement between God and Christian people.

* * *

Blessed be Thou, O Lord. With Thy omnipresent mercy look upon this assembly of Thy ministers. With Thy omniscient grace hear our prayers of adoration, thanksgiving, confession, and supplication. With Thy omnipotent wisdom guide and direct the course of this gathering. With Thy unfailing compassion wilt Thou accept our sacrifices of rededication and consecration to the cause of Jesus Christ. Henceforth let us not be slaves of sin, but slaves of righteousness for sanctification, for we have been buried with him, and we have been raised to his glory. Let Thy word speak to us. Let us preach his word. Glory be to the Christ our savior, now and evermore. Amen.

NOTE: "Omnipresent" means present in all places, "omniscient" denotes all-knowing, and "omnipotent" indicates having complete authority.

* * *

Praised, extolled, exalted, and sanctified be Thy name. With Thy unfailing mercy look upon the assembly of Thy ministers, and let the light of Thy incarnate word illumine their souls. Let Thy will be done on earth! Let Thy will be done through eternity! Amen.

NOTE: "Incarnate" means personified or made in human flesh.

Speaker

Praised, magnified, sanctified, exalted, and extolled be Thy name, O Thou, creator of the universe and father of mankind. As Thou hast placed order in the universe, so hast Thou paved the way of salvation, that a sinner might become a saint. We thank Thee for this Thy grace. But, O Lord, realizing our own faults and inadequacies as Thy ministers, humbly do we bring ourselves to Thee for fresh consecration to the high ends of Thy ministry. Wilt Thou cleanse us according to Thy will. And now we thank Thee for Thy providence which has brought us our distinguished speaker. Wilt Thou be with him, as he speaks to us, and bless and inspire each one of us as we listen to him. We thank Thee for this Christian fellowship of like-minded ministers. Let Thy wisdom prevail over human knowledge, and let all of our academic endeavors glorify the Christ, in whose name we pray. Amen.

* * *

Praised be Thou, O Lord, for this assembly of Thy ministers. Though we are unworthy of Thy call, humbly do we bow before Thee. Be merciful unto us as we bring ourselves to Thee for fresh consecration to the high ends of Thy kingdom. Be gracious unto all churches who speak unto Thee. We thank Thee for this distinguished minister whom Thou hast brought to us this morning. We thank Thee for his many activities as minister, lecturer, and author. But, above all, we thank Thee for his eminent Christian leadership among the churches of the world. Father, bless him as he speaks to us, and bless us according to Thy will, as we listen to him. Glory be to the cross, now and evermore. Amen.

O Lord, mighty and merciful, it was Thy potent word that turned back the sea of reeds. It was Thy potent word that withheld the waters of the Jordan. It was Thy potent word that has become flesh in the savior of mankind. We thank Thee for the mystery of the power of Thy grace which turns sinners into saints, which propels believers unto nonbelievers, and which gives victory over death. As Thou hast ordered the universe to be and to become, so may Thy gospel order the lives of all children of man. Instill within us that potency and that mystery of active peace which Thou alone canst give. Through Jesus Christ, our lord. Amen.

NOTE: The Red Sea is called "sea of reeds" in the Hebrew Bible. As God created the universe by His word, so by His incarnate word He creates a saint out of a sinner. "Peace" in the Bible has a much more active sense than in English.

RURAL CHURCH INSTITUTE

Our Father, mighty and merciful, humbly do we bow before Thee at the beginning of this another session of our gathering, and thank Thee for the saving grace and redeeming mercy of the Christ. We thank Thee for the simplicity of rural life, and its relation to the New Testament Christianity. Help us to realize the significance of Thy house in maintaining our ideals and expanding Thy kingdom. May Thy tabernacle be exalted above all that which is good, true, and beautiful in the mundane world. In Jesus' name we pray. Amen.

SCRIPTURES: 2 Sam. 7:1-11; Hag. 1:2-8.

NOTE: To a total stranger, who travels through this blessed land, two distinct welcome signs are the towering steeple of the church and the imposing belfry of the school, especially in the rural area. Alas, these signs gradually disappear when a city grows.

GROUND BREAKING

Praised be Thou, O Lord, for Thy word incarnate, in whom we live, move, and have our being. We thank Thee for this dawn of another day in the chronicle of this Thy own congregation. May the foundation of Thy new house of worship be a veritable rock of salvation. May the rise of Thy new house of prayer declare the glory of Thy handiwork. May the ministry of Thy new house of assembly become the fountain of living water to the saints and sages of tomorrow. We rededicate ourselves to Thy cause, O Lord. With Thy abundant mercy bless us as Thou wilt. In our savior's name we pray. Amen.

> NOTE: Acts 17:28 says in part: ". . . in him we live and move, and have our being. . . ." The house of worship is often called "house of prayer" or "house of assembly" in Judeo-Christian literature. In Hebrew and Greek, the word for "house" sometimes means family or household.

DEDICATION OF A NEW UNIT

Come Thou, almighty God. Look down upon the handiwork of Thy children. Amid the threats of impending war and the despair of the suffering of the righteous throughout the world, we acknowledge Thy providence that has placed us in this blessed land of liberty. In gratitude, do we dedicate to Thee these humble fruits of our labor, and thank Thee for the devoted thought, consecrated skill, and contributed material that have enabled us to magnify this Thy house of worship. May through the portals of this new unit Thy shepherds guide the flock to the fountain of living water. May within the portals of the new chapel the divine peace of sweet communion dispel the darkness of earthly faults. O Lord, in utmost humility do we place ourselves in Thy hands as a living sacrifice. May the deathless cross shine through us unto the utmost parts of Thy creation. In our savior's name we pray. Amen.

NOTE: Written in the spring of 1941.

DINNER

Word—Wisdom

Praised be Thou, O Lord, for Thy love and mercy gathered us together about these tables. We thank Thee for Thy word incarnate, who speaks to us here tonight, as he spake along the shores of Galilee. We thank Thee for Thy divine wisdom which speaks unto us tonight, as she spake in the streets of Jerusalem. Let us hear Thy word. Let us listen to Thy wisdom whisper. Bless the food and this fellowship according to Thy will, and make us Thine, now and forevermore. Amen.

SCRIPTURES: Prov. 8:1-4; Mark 1:14-28; John 1:14.

Promotion

O Lord, because of our consciousness of Thy presence, we bow before Thee. Because of our feeling of Thy assured guidance, we thank Thee. Because of the awareness of our weakness, we beseech Thee. We thank Thee because of the constant growth of this Thy house of worship. We beseech Thee because of the plans that lie before us. May this blessed Christian fellowship now about these tables be not in vain. May we receive a positive command, as we listen to our distinguished speaker tonight. May we make ourselves vitally useful for the cause of the Christ, to whom be glory forever and ever. Amen.

NOTE: "House of worship" refers to the church building. Some Jewish synagogues bear this name, though the phrase is expressed in Hebrew.

Worship

INVOCATION

Come Thou, almighty God. The heavens and the earth praise Thee. Command, O God of hosts, as we humbly bow before Thee. By virtue of our trust in Thee, we surrender to Thee our flesh, our blood, yea, our all. Open our spiritual eyes so that we may behold Thy countenance. Open our spiritual ears so that we may hear Thy voice. In our savior's name we pray. Amen.

* * *

We wait for Thee, O Lord. Let us rededicate ourselves to Thy cause. We wait for Thee, O Lord. Let us behold Thy countenance. We wait for Thee, O Lord. Let us hear Thy voice. We wait for Thee, O Lord. Let us renew our faith in Thy word. Bless this assembly according to Thy will. Amen.

* * *

Come Thou, blessed Lord. With Thy unfailing mercy look upon this assembly of Thy ministers. Accept their sacrifices of rededication and reconsecration to Thy cause, and let Thy will be done on earth even as it is in heaven. Be with us, O Lord, as we worship Thee. Amen.

> NOTE: All servants of God are "ministers." Therefore, all Christians should be ministers.

* * *
37

We wait for Thee, O Lord. May we renew our strength. We wait for Thee, O Lord. May we rekindle our faith. We wait for Thee, O Lord. May we behold Thy countenance. We wait for Thee, O Lord. May we hear Thy voice. We wait for Thee, O Lord. May we feel the touch of Thy hand. May this act of worship be acceptable in Thy sight, O God, our redeemer and our savior. Amen.

*   *   *

O Thou, rock, shield, and redeemer of the righteous, grant, we pray, that we walk in Thy light. May our prayers of adoration, thanksgiving, confession, and supplication be acceptable in Thy sight. Bless this gathering and enable us to glorify Thy incarnate word. Amen.

*   *   *

Come Thou, almighty God. Look down upon this assembly of Thy servants. With humble hearts and contrite spirits, do we approach the golden throne of Thy presence. May our rededication to the cause of the Christ be acceptable in Thy sight, O Lord, Lord of lords, King of kings. In our savior's name we pray. Amen.

* * *

Come Thou, almighty God, Father of mankind. With Thy abundant mercy and ever-present love, look upon this assembly of Thy children. Hear their prayers of confession, their supplications of faith, and their songs of praise. Be with us and bless us according to Thy will, O Lord. We ask through Jesus, the Christ. Amen.

* * *

Come Thou, almighty God. The heavens and the earth praise Thee. Command, O God of hosts, as we humbly bow before Thee. May Thy tabernacle be exalted upon the holy hill, may Thy people walk in Thy divine light, and may Thy kingdom descend upon Thy wondrous creation. Grant us that grace, that faith, and that peace which belong to the shepherd of shepherds, even Jesus Christ. Amen.

Thanksgiving

Magnified, exalted, and sanctified be Thy name, O Lord God, for Thou hast given us this day of Thanksgiving. As David of ancient Israel, so do we, as sons and daughters of true Israel, even as disciples of the Christ, assemble here to praise Thy majesty and magnificence. May Thy infinite mercy render this act of worship acceptable in Thy sight. In our savior's name we pray. Amen.

SCRIPTURES: 2 Sam. 7:27-29; Gal. 6:16; Heb. 8:8.

PASTORAL PRAYER

General

O Thou, mighty God, merciful God, the Lord of space, the Lord of time, and the ruler of the world in which we live, we praise Thy name. We thank Thee for the Christ and his church, for his gospel and his ministry, for the saints and sages of the past, and for disciples and ministers of today and tomorrow. With humble hearts and contrite spirits, we confess before Thy throne of glory our faults and transgressions as members of Thy household. But Thou knowest all, O Lord. We rededicate our all to Thee as a living sacrifice. Awake our souls from the scarlet couches of complacency, and cleanse them whiter than snow, and render them purer than the lily of the valley. Put Thy Holy Spirit upon us. Inspire us. Strengthen us when we are weary. Sustain us when we fall. Guard us when we face the forces of evil. But use us according to Thy will. Father, bless Thy church. May all nations flow unto the spiritual hill of Zion. May all peoples follow in the footsteps of our master, even Jesus Christ. In his name we pray. Amen.

NOTE: "Name" means person. "In his name" then means through the person of Jesus Christ.

* * *

May Thy name be praised, O Lord. I confess my ignorance as to the nature of the soul's cry of those who have gathered here in Thy presence, but I know that Thou art omniscient. Wilt Thou hearken to their prayers, and bless them according to Thy will. Draw us ever closer and nearer to the Christ, as we worship Thee. In his name we pray. Amen.

NOTE: "Name" means person in the above prayer.

* * *

O Thou, light of the world, from the shadow of our daily burden, humbly do we draw near unto Thy light trusting in Thy mercy unto us. We thank Thee for this peace and comfort which flow into our hearts, as we thus communicate with Thee. We place ourselves in Thy hand, and we find ourselves in Thy care. We behold Thy glorious countenance, and we sense Thy grace upon us. We listen to Thy divine voice, and we are healed by Thy love. For this mystery we thank Thee, O Lord. Help us to learn to live near unto Thee, and embrace the beauty of Thy holiness. We ask through Jesus Christ, our Lord. Amen.

NOTE: As in English, "hand" means power or authority in Greek and Hebrew, in some passages of the Bible.

* * *

Come Thou, almighty God. The heavens and the earth praise Thee. Command, O God of hosts, as we humbly bow before Thee. By virtue of our trust in Thy promise we now surrender to Thee our flesh, our blood, yea, our all. Wilt Thou bless this assembly of Thy children, and others who were unable to come. May Thy tabernacle be exalted upon Thy holy hill. May Thy people walk in Thy divine light. May Thy kingdom descend upon Thy wondrous creation. Grant, O Lord, to those innocent and courageous throughout the world who suffer today for Thy name's sake, that grace, that faith, and that peace which Thou alone canst give. Through Jesus Christ, our lord. Amen.

*   *   *

O Lord, our Lord, how wonderful is Thy name. Though the day is dark, let us realize that the sun, the moon, and the stars shine behind the clouds. So as we bring ourselves to Thee from the shadow of our daily burden for fresh consecration to the high ends of Thy kingdom, let Thy countenance shine upon us. Wilt Thou bless each one in Thy presence. Heal the sick, strengthen the weak, comfort the sorrowful, and guide the perplexed, and let us each feel the touch of Thy hand of mercy. Let us go forth from this Thy house of prayer with our faith confirmed and with our spirit renewed to serve Thee. Through Jesus Christ, our lord, we pray. Amen.

*   *   *

Come Thou, almighty God. The cedars of Lebanon praise Thee. The roses of Sharon adore Thee. The heavens and the earth worship Thee. We confess before Thee our steadfast faith in Thy word incarnate, and thank Thee for Thy redeeming love. We pray that Thou wilt watch over these children as they participate in this worship. Bless them, our Father, as they listen to the proclamation of the gospel; and enlighten them with Thy word. With mercy accept their rededication to Thy cause, and re-create others who confess the name of Christ. Glory be unto Thee, O God, forever and ever. Amen.

NOTE: "Gospel" means good news.

* * *

O Thou, creator of the universe and Father of mankind, we thank Thee for these precious moments of prayer when we may communicate with Thee. Hear our humble words of adoration, confession, thanksgiving, and supplication. May our thoughts be cleansed, may our words be purified, and may our deeds become acceptable in Thy sight. Draw us nearer to the perfect image of the Christ. In his name we pray. Amen.

* * *

Almighty God, Father of our good shepherd, even Jesus Christ, may Thy name be praised for this communion of the saints. We confess our steadfast faith in that good shepherd, who leaves the ninety-nine to seek the one that is lost. Bless all members of Thy holy household, those who are in Thy presence here, and others who are absent. Like rain unto parched land, may Thy grace renew our lives; like water unto thirsty souls, may Thy love heal our sorrows; like bread unto hungry persons, may Thy mercy sustain our faith. Let the beam of Thy shining cross penetrate our souls, and let us truly feel the warmth of its glow. To that ancient cross be glory forever and ever. Amen.

> NOTE: The simile of the good shepherd appears in Matt. 18:12-14; Luke 15:4-7.

* * *

O Lord, our Lord, Lord of all mankind, we thank Thee for our glorious consciousness of Thy presence in the temporal darkness of human turmoil. Towering above the mundane chaos of vanities and transgressions, let there arise within us Christian faith, hope, and love. Bless this church, its minister, his family, its officers, their families, its other members, their families, and those other members of Thy household here and abroad. Be with us as we worship Thee, and grant us that silent power of truth that has become flesh in Jesus Christ, in whose name we pray. Amen.

* * *

Praised be Thou, O Lord, creator of the universe and Father of mankind. In these precious moments of prayer, humbly do we approach Thy golden throne of grace, and we thank Thee for this hour of worship and for the ministry of the Christ. Wilt Thou dispel our rebellious thoughts and stubborn minds, and let us sense and acknowledge here and now something greater than the law of Moses, for Christ died for us. As the new creation of the Christ, let us each bear the marks of his salvation. As we bless Thy name, so wilt Thou bless those who hearken to the gospel proclaimed. Lead us on, O king eternal. Let us walk in Thy light. In Jesus' name we pray. Amen.

*   *   *

O Lord, mighty and merciful, we thank Thee for the saints and sages of the past, who by virtue of their faith saw the unseen, heard the inaudible, sensed the supernatural, and proclaimed the good news of salvation. We thank Thee for that faith of our fathers. Let us embrace anew that faith which enabled them to perceive the ultimate cause of what we see, hear, and feel. Put Thy spirit upon us, and let us preach Thy gospel in word and in deed. Be gracious unto us and hear our prayers. Grant Thy grace of healing and comfort to those who are in need, and use us according to Thy will. In our savior's name we pray. Amen.

*   *   *

O Lord, creator and ruler of the universe, and savior and Father of mankind in whose presence we live, move, and have our being, we praise Thy name for Thou hast brought us together to this house of prayer. As we participate in this worship, be merciful unto us, and grant us spiritual eyes to behold Thy countenance, spiritual ears to hear Thy word preached, and spiritual sense to discern Thy presence. Wilt Thou make Thyself real to us as we walk with the Christ. We would thank Thee for every step we take, and every breath we breathe. Glory be to the Christ, in whose name we pray. Amen.

* * *

Glorified and sanctified be Thy name, O Lord, our God and our redeemer. We thank Thee for the return of this day of our Lord and for our own return to this Thy house of prayer. As we participate in this act of worship, help us to ascend the spiritual hill of Zion from the world of human life, to a genuine faithful communion with Thee from a mere good social habit, and to the sincere rededication of ourselves to Thy cause from the complacency of self-justification. Thus, let us lose ourselves in Thee as a living sacrifice. Glory be to the ancient cross, now and forevermore. Amen.

* * *

Praised be Thou, O Lord, creator of the universe, who hast made man in Thy own image and likeness. We thank Thee for these golden moments of prayer, when we speak to Thee, and when we hear Thy voice. We thank Thee for Thy precious gift to us, even Jesus Christ. We confess and confirm our steadfast faith in him. Bless those who worship Thee according to Thy will, and accept the sacrifice of those who rededicate themselves to Thy cause. Wilt Thou guard and guide those who are absent, heal and comfort those who are sick, and strengthen and console those who are bereaved. Implant in our hearts the ancient cross, and let us embrace that peace which Thou alone canst give. In Jesus' name. Amen.

> NOTE: Gen. 1:26 says in part: "Let us make man in our image, after our likeness. . . ." The Hebrew word for "image" may signify the external form, and that for "likeness" the internal relation.

Restoration of the Church

Praised be Thou, O Lord, creator of the universe and Father of mankind. Thou hast ordained the church of Jesus Christ and nurtured its destiny from the magnificent past of Thy creation to the glorious future of its victory. Wilt Thou forgive our sins and cleanse us anew. Put Thy spirit upon us, and let us speak Thy word boldly, as in the days of apostles. May the ancient church come, and may it lead us to the fulfillment of Thy will on earth. Wilt Thou hear our prayers. Speak, O Lord, as we are Thine to serve the Christ. In his name we pray. Amen.

Ministry

Mighty God and merciful Father, blessed be Thou, O Lord, for Thou hast brought us together to worship Thee. We pray that Thou wilt bless us according to Thy will, as we rededicate ourselves to Thy cause. Wilt Thou cleanse us, remold us, and re-create us, so that our ministry may become more acceptable in Thy sight. But, Oh, great healer of the sick and wondrous comforter of those who are in despair and sorrow, be gracious unto them, especially those within our fellowship, and make them whole in body and in spirit. Now we ask that Thou wilt mercifully send Thy peace to all mankind, and let them hear Thy gospel of salvation, for the world is Thine, through Jesus Christ, our Lord. Glory be to his name, now and forevermore. Amen.

Minister

O Lord, our Lord and our savior, we praise Thy name. Human words are incapable of describing Thee. Human creeds are not able to confine Thee. Human doctrines cannot fully express Thy nature. Yet we thank Thee for our childlike faith which tells us that whenever and wherever those who believe gather Thou art there. So we look up unto Thee and thank Thee for that faith and that knowledge which tell us that Thou art indeed our savior and redeemer. We thank Thee for Thy messenger of this hour. Speak to us through him. Grant us Thy wisdom and confirm our faith in the Christ, and enable us to give ourselves more fully to Thy cause to the end that more of our souls may be filled by Thy word. In our savior's name. Amen.

*   *   *

O Thou, Lord of creation, king of the universe, and Father of mankind, we praise Thy name for the gift of the Christ to all sons and daughters of man. We thank Thee for Christ's saving grace and redeeming love. As we confess our steadfast faith in him, wilt Thou hear our prayers and supplications, and those of other Christian men and women throughout the world. Let Thy breath strengthen the weak and heal the sick. Let Thy hand raise the fallen and guard the faithful. May Thy spirit rest upon us, especially the minister of this hour, and may the light of Thy word illumine our pathway toward the ancient cross. In Jesus' name. Amen.

*   *   *

Blessed be Thou, O Lord, creator of the universe and Father of mankind. We thank Thee for Thy gracious providence that has brought us together to worship Thee, for Christ's tender ministry that has given us Thy peace, and for these golden moments of prayer when we may communicate with Thee. Bless all who speak to Thee, according to Thy will. Open our ears and let us hear Thy voice. Open our eyes and let us behold Thy countenance. And through this mystic communion let us realize the power of prayer. Grant to our minister that courage, that wisdom, and that insight, which Thou alone canst give, as he speaks to us. To the ancient cross be glory forever and ever. Amen.

*   *   *

May Thy name be praised, O Lord of the universe and Father of mankind. We thank Thee for Thy steadfast love that has brought us together to worship Thee. As we humbly approach Thy golden throne of holiness, hear our prayers of confession and supplication. Bless this Thy congregation according to Thy will, especially our minister and his family, and our guests and visitors in Thy presence. May Thy guiding spirit rest upon our guest minister and make him speak Thy word. Grant us all that faith and that courage, with which to press on toward the higher goal of life. Through Jesus Christ, our lord. Amen.

> NOTE: "Steadfast love" is one recent translation of the Hebrew word which is frequently rendered "mercy." Neither translation gives fully the profound meaning of this word. "Religious love" or "religious mercy" may give a better sense.

*   *   *

51

Blessed be Thou, O Lord, Lord of salvation, who delivered ancient Israel from the bondage in Egypt, and who, through the Christ, saves Thy children from the fetters of death; we praise Thy name. We thank Thee for Thy providence which has brought us together to worship Thee, and also for Thy messenger whom Thou hast sent to us. Wilt Thou hearken to our soul's cry and respond to us according to Thy will. Be with this Thy messenger, as he speaks to us. Though we are unable to see Thee face to face, may Thy spirit enable us to hear Thy voice. So may this act of worship become truly an act of sacred communion with Thee. Let us lose ourselves in Thy gracious care, now and forevermore. In Jesus' name. Amen.

*   *   *

O Thou, ruler of the universe and Father of mankind, in whose mysterious presence we live, move, and have our being, we praise Thy name for Thy gift of our savior, and we confess our steadfast faith in him. We thank Thee for these precious moments to speak to Thee and hear Thy voice. We pray that Thou wilt accept the prayers of adoration, confession, thanksgiving, and petition, of all of Thy faithful servants here and abroad. We thank Thee for Thy messenger whom Thou hast sent to us. Wilt Thou bless him, as he speaks to us, and may his words become a blessing to us. As we rededicate ourselves to Thy cause, wilt Thou use us according to Thy will for the glory of Jesus Christ. In his name we pray. Amen.

*   *   *

O God, our Father, we thank Thee for Thy providence which has gathered us together to worship Thee. Thy commandments and statutes, we have read. Thy doctrine, we have heard. Christ's word, we have accepted. Thy gracious salvation, we have experienced. We have no words to speak to Thee, but pray that Thou wilt accept our praise, prayers, and supplications from our hearts. Father, cleanse us and re-create us according to Thy will, so that we may become more useful in the ministry of our blessed lord. We thank Thee for Thy messenger of this morning. Be with him, as he speaks; and as we leave this house of prayer, let us feel that we have been drawn truly another step closer to the golden throne of the Christ. In his name we pray. Amen.

*   *   *

Come Thou, almighty God, God of the universe and Father of mankind. With Thy abundant grace look upon this assembly of Thy children. Wilt Thou accept our heartfelt praise and humble thanksgiving, and hear our sincere confession and earnest supplication. Bless, O Lord, each person present here. Bless our minister and his family, and bless our visiting minister for this service. May Thy guiding, sustaining, comforting, and healing hand be upon all believers, and enable them to share that peace which Thou alone canst give. Through Jesus Christ, our savior, we pray. Amen.

Nature

Lord of the universe and Father of mankind, for the renewal of life within Thy own creation, and for the conquest of death by Thy holy son, we thank Thee. Let us truly worship Thee with heartfelt confession and thanksgiving. With utmost joy and steadfast peace, may our souls soar like the birds of heaven, may our hearts blossom like the lilies of the field, and may our song of praise rise unto Thee like the sweet incense of old. Let us hear Thy word proclaimed, O God. There is none beside Thee. In Jesus' name we pray. Amen.

Spring

Humbly do we bow before Thee, O Lord, confessing our faith in Thy word incarnate. We thank Thee for the cross, symbol of sacrifice and salvation. We thank Thee for Thy love, token of purity and perfection. May the songs of birds and smiles of flowers enhance our devotion to the cause, for which the Christ was sent to mankind. Let us rededicate ourselves to Thee for that cause, as we truly listen to the proclamation of the gospel of the Christ, in whose name we pray. Amen.

*   *   *

O Lord, our savior and our Father, from the shadow of our daily burden, humbly do we approach the light of Thy presence. We thank Thee for the return of the spring and the return of Thy faithful believers to Thy house of worship. As we participate in this act of worship, let Thy light descend upon us, and let us realize that it is not enough to know the Christ by merely hearing and reading about him, but we should truly experience his presence. So breathe upon us, and let us sense the touch of Thy spirit. Thus may our souls be revived, so that we may faithfully serve the Christ. Praised be Thou, O Lord, now and evermore. Amen.

Summer

Our Lord, and our Father, Thy everlasting love has brought us here on this beautiful day of the summer, and we thank Thee for this opportunity to worship Thee as Thy own children. As we participate in this worship, may this house of prayer become the sanctuary of holy thoughts and sincere devotion to Thy cause. May Thy hand of fatherly love touch our souls, as Thy good news is proclaimed. Glory be to the cross of Jesus world without end. In his name we pray. Amen.

NOTE: "Good news" is another expression for gospel.

Magnified and exalted be Thy name, O God of the universe and Father of mankind. With utmost faith in Thy only begotten son, do we assemble here to worship Thee. We thank Thee for the many varied gifts of Thy Holy Spirit. Though we are not alike in talents, abilities, and occupations, help us to realize the oneness of Thy church. Like colorful autumnal leaves, let us be woven into the unity of the golden brocade of Thy household, each contributing much to its beautiful unity. Let us love one another as Thy children, and may Thy peace reign over us now and evermore. Amen.

*   *   *

Praised, magnified, and exalted be Thy name, O Lord, our God and our Father. In the beauty of the golden brocade of autumnal leaves, humbly do we approach Thy throne of grace with thankful hearts and contrite spirits—thankful hearts for Thou hast granted us this another hour of worship, contrite spirits as we realize our own faults and transgressions. Particularly do we thank Thee for Thy messenger whom Thou hast sent to us. We thank Thee for his consecrated ministry and gracious leadership. Wilt Thou bless him as he speaks to us. As Thou art, so Christ is. As Christ is, so let us become. We are Thine, O Lord, cleanse us and use us to the end that the ancient church might be reestablished on earth. Glory be to the Christ, world without end. Amen.

*   *   *

Glory be unto Thee, O Father of all mankind, for the shining heavenly stars above, for the colorful autumnal leaves below, for the innocent sleep of a babe, for the vigorous activities of the young, and for the quiet repose of the aged. Grant us the spiritual insight that we may discern Thy potent wisdom which manifests itself in every sphere of the universe. May that divine wisdom guide us throughout this assembly, and may we truly sense Thy presence among us. To this end, and to the end that the ministry of the Christ be established and exalted, do we invoke Thy blessing upon us. Hear us now, as we pray in the words of our blessed lord: Our Father in heaven, hallowed be Thy name. Thy kingdom come. Thy will be done on earth as it is in heaven. Give us this day our daily bread, and forgive us our debts as we forgive our debtors. Lead us not into temptation, but deliver us from evil. For Thine is the kingdom, and the power, and the glory. Forever and ever. Amen.

NOTE: The doxology of the Lord's prayer is not found in the leading manuscripts of the New Testament.

Magnified and exalted be Thy name, our heavenly Father, for Thou hast brought us together to worship Thee. We thank Thee for the unfathomable power which Thou hast enshrined in the universe and for the wondrous virtue which Thou hast bestowed upon man through Jesus Christ. We confess that from time to time we have gone astray, we have stumbled, we have forgotten our mission and ministry, and thus we have sinned. Lord, cleanse us again as we submit ourselves to Thee. Let us serve Thee by serving Thy children, and let us prepare the way for the advent of the Christ. Though the snow and ice encompass us without, let Thy love and grace warm our hearts within. Be merciful unto those who suffer this day mentally or physically, and let Thy peace prevail over us, world without end. In Jesus' name we pray. Amen.

> NOTE: "Name" signifies person. In Judaism "the Name" means God.

* * *

O Thou, God of mercy, God of love, God of salvation, Father of Christ, and Father of mankind, we praise Thy name. We thank Thee for the purity of the snow without and the innocence of the saved soul within. We thank Thee for this opportunity to gather together to praise Thee, to thank Thee, to confess unto Thee, and to supplicate unto Thee. Especially do we thank Thee for Thy minister of the morning, for his leadership, for his words, and for his acts. Wilt Thou open our hearts to Thy word which comes to us through him. Hear the prayers of all of Thy ministers throughout the world, and draw us together to the unity found in the Christ. In his name we pray. Amen.

Our Father in heaven, we thank Thee for the glowing star of ancient Bethlehem. We thank Thee for the silent power of Thy ordered universe. We thank Thee for Thy holy love of Jesus Christ. May the golden brocade with a woof of silent power and a warp of holy love be woven within our conscience, and may that golden brocade impel us to find joy in sharing pain, hunger, distress, and despair of all mankind. Wilt Thou nourish the unfailing virtues of Christian manhood and womanhood to the end that we may at last manifest that silent power and holy love which have become flesh in Thy only begotten son. Amen.

*   *   *

O creator of the universe, for the sun of Thy glory over Jerusalem, for the moon of Thy wisdom over Carmel, and for the star of Thy intelligence over Bethlehem, we thank Thee. As we participate in this worship, may it be the star of hope that leads us to Thy perfect peace. Let it prevail over us, O Lord. Let Thy peace prevail over mankind now and evermore. Amen.

NOTE: "Peace" in the Bible means not only the cessation of war, but also safety, healthiness, completeness, or perfection.

New Year

Our gracious Father, who hast ordained seasons and years, and who hast created man in Thy own image and likeness, we most humbly bow before Thee at the beginning of this new year with the sense of seriousness of the commission that Thou hast given to us to bear the ark of the New Testament even unto the uttermost parts of the world that Thou hast prepared for us. With shame we look upon the days gone by, for we were not ready and caused Thee to "break out upon us," but now we are determined to carry on with renewed faith, hope, and love. Awaken our consciousness to the fact that we are living souls. Create in us the perception of Christian duties and responsibilities. Enable us to sanctify ourselves to Thee and Thy only son, to whom be glory forever and ever. Amen.

SCRIPTURES: 1 Chron. 15:12-15; Matt. 28:18-20.

THE LORD'S TABLE

General

O Lord, let the heavens sing and the earth rejoice, for Thou hast given us Jesus, the Christ. We thank Thee for the ancient cross signifying the Christ's conquest over death and for this holy emblem confirming our trust in Thy saving grace. As we participate in this sacred feast, let there arise within us a renewed sense of faith, hope, and love. May Thy counsel endure from the rising of the sun even unto its setting. Glory be to the Christ, in whose name we pray. Amen.

*   *   *

Mighty God and merciful Father, we thank Thee for this renewal of our precious covenant with Thee, and for this reaffirmation of our victorious faith in the Christ. Enable us to surrender ourselves unto Thee, that we might gain the spiritual power with which to resist evil and the divine wisdom with which to practice righteousness. Let us remember Thee every moment in holy anticipation of the life eternal. Through Jesus Christ, our lord. Amen.

*   *   *

Praised be Thou, O Lord, for Thou art the healer, comforter, sustainer, and savior of all mankind. We thank Thee for Thy exceeding mercy which enables us to participate in this feast of the new covenant. As we partake of this emblem, let every element of our existence rejoin in this divine mystery, let every fiber of our being respond to Thy call, and let our hearts and minds indeed find refuge in Thy word incarnate. To him be glory forever and ever. Amen.

> NOTE: The Greek word for disposition, will, or testament, is often translated "covenant" in the New Testament. The primary meaning of the Hebrew word translated "covenant" is an agreement between two parties, e.g., between God and Israel.

* * *

Mighty God, merciful Father, we thank Thee for this communion with Thee, for this communion with the Christ, and for this communion with the saints. As Thou hast given us the Christ, so let us give ourselves unto Thee. As Jesus died in our behalf, so let us lay down our lives for Thy cause. Enable us to share the burden of the cross in Christian love and peace, to the end that we may rise again in the newness of life. In Jesus' name we pray. Amen.

> NOTE: Early Christians were sometimes called "saints" in the New Testament.

* * *

Heavenly Father, let us flee for these few moments from the troubled world, so that we may again embrace the vision of the cross. We seek not the way of escape, but we do seek the faith and courage with which to face the tasks and duties before us. May we truly sense Thy presence, as we partake of this sacred feast. In our savior's name we pray. Amen.

* * *

God of mercy, God of love, we thank Thee for these precious moments when we may recapture the ultimate glory of our faith in Christ Jesus. May this sacred emblem instill within us hearts, minds, and attitudes as clean as the blue sky and as pure as the white clouds. May Thy golden throne in heaven cast its beauty upon our lives here on earth. In our savior's name we pray. Amen.

* * *

Holy, holy, holy, O Lord of hosts, Thy glory fills this house of worship, as we approach those golden moments of sacred communion. Humbly do we partake of these precious emblems, with thanksgiving for Thy eternal grace and with confession of our utter unworthiness. Mercifully hearken to our prayers, and cleanse us of our selfish hearts and unclean lips. Let us truly proclaim the light of life, for Thou alone art the fountain of life. Through Jesus Christ, our lord. Amen.

SCRIPTURE: Isa. 6:3-5.

*   *   *

God of might, God of grace, and God of love, in the fleeting tide of human life, wilt Thou arrest our meaningless concern here and now. Let us recall Thy gospel, envision the cross, and participate in this communion. But, O Lord, our sins are grave. Our souls are unclean. Yet we know and believe that Jesus alone is our savior. Thou hast given him to us. He died for us. We have gained our hope for eternal life. So humbly do we surrender ourselves to Thy care. We thank Thee for these golden moments. Mercifully accept our living sacrifice. Glory be to the mystery and miracle of this ordinance. Through Jesus Christ we pray. Amen.

*   *   *

O Thou, comforter, healer, and savior of mankind, as we approach these sacred moments, we cannot but realize our own unworthiness for this wonderful grace. Lord, cleanse us of our worldly thoughts and manners of life, and let the rod and staff of the great shepherd lead us. May the heavenly flesh of the Christ replace our earthly flesh, and his innocent blood replace our sinful blood. And so may the golden throne in heaven cast its shadow upon our pathway here on earth. In our savior's name we pray. Amen.

> NOTE: The "rod" in Ps. 23:4 is to be used to ward off any danger that may menace the flock, and the "staff" in this verse is for guiding the flock.

*   *   *

Glory be unto Thee, O Lord, for Thou hast given us Christ Jesus, the great shepherd of the sheep. We thank Thee for this reenactment of his memorable feast. As the ancient cross signifies his victory over death, so may our partaking of this blessed emblem mean our sharing in the life eternal. We yield ourselves unto Thee, in order that we may find ourselves in Thy care. We look up unto Thee, in order that we may sense Thy grace. We incline our ears unto Thee, in order that we may hear Thy voice. May the beauty of Thy holiness prevail in our hearts now and evermore. Amen.

*   *   *

O Lord, Lord of the universe, our Lord, there is none beside Thee. We thank Thee for Thy word incarnate, even Jesus Christ. In memory of his victorious deed and saving grace, do we participate in this holy feast. May the ancient cross illumine our souls. May this sacred emblem warm our hearts. May we truly rejoin the fold of Thy sheep Grant us peace. We pray in Jesus' name. Amen.

*   *   *

O Thou, Lord of mercy, Lord of grace, we thank Thee for Thy own image in Jesus Christ, and for this token of his redeeming love. May this reenactment of his last supper signify the reaffirmation of our faith in him. May this renewal of the new covenant mean the reawakening of our souls. May our realization of Thy omnipresence denote the revitalization of our Christian fellowship. Let Thy rod and Thy staff sustain us, as we humbly walk in the footsteps of our master, and let the ancient cross illumine our hearts now and forevermore. In our savior's name we pray. Amen.

NOTE: "New Covenant" of 2 Cor. 3:14 is rendered "New Testament" in the King James Version of 1611. "Rod" and "staff" appear in Ps. 23:4.

*   *   *

O Thou, light of the world, we thank Thee for these golden moments of the hour of worship. As we partake of these precious emblems, let us truly meditate upon the majesty of Thy mighty act and upon the wonder of Christ's saving grace. Though our days pass like a shadow, may our faith abide forever. Though our years slip away like a dream, may the church stand forever. We pray through Jesus Christ, our lord. Amen.

*   *   *

O Thou, God of Israel, our Lord, and our Father, Thou hast given us Thy only son, and he has saved us by his grace. By faith in Thy living word, and by act according to Thy ordinance, our sins were pardoned, and we were reborn as Thy children. We thank Thee for this miracle of all miracles. May every word and every act in this memorial feast of the death and resurrection of our blessed savior become a witness and testimony to the one, holy, catholic, and apostolic church. May glory be to the cross of Jesus forever and ever. Amen.

*   *   *

Praised be Thou, O Lord, for Christ's victory over death, for his gift of the new covenant, and for his saving grace unto all mankind. With thankful hearts and contrite spirits, do we partake of this holy emblem, and we pray that this our act of participation in the enactment of his memorial feast will truly render that which is temporal to permanent, that which is perishable to imperishable, and that which is mortal to immortal. May the power of Thy mystery manifest itself in our hearts, now and evermore. Amen.

* * *

Blessed be Thou, O Lord, creator of the universe and redeemer of mankind. We thank Thee for the divine victory over death and for the human urge for perfection. As we partake of this heavenly emblem, may that which is divine and that which is human unite by Thy grace. And may that unity blossom into the flower of eternal peace which Thou alone canst give. In our savior's name we pray. Amen.

* * *

Our heavenly Father, we thank Thee for these precious moments of Thy grace which has brought us to this table of the new covenant. As we partake of this sacred emblem, may it truly remold our souls. Let it supplant our doubt with faith, despair with hope, ill will with love, and strife with peace. May Thy guiding star ever illumine the pathway of life, now and evermore. Amen.

*   *   *

O Thou, author of signs and wonders, Thou hast revealed Thyself in Christ Jesus, and hast given him to the world of sinfulness and bewilderment. He became obedient to death in order that even we might be saved. He gained victory over death in order that even we might share the eternal life. And now, O Lord, by Thy grace we are gathered here to renew our new covenant with Thee. Remembering the past miracle of the gift of Thy son, and anticipating the future miracle of the actualization of Thy word, we do humbly wait upon the manifestation of our blessed savior. Wilt Thou make us ready to meet him. In his name we pray. Amen.

*   *   *

O Thou, Lord of mercy, Father of love, we thank Thee for Thy own image and likeness in Jesus Christ, and his saving grace and redeeming sacrifice for our sake. As we participate in this feast of the new covenant, wilt Thou bless these emblems; and as we rededicate ourselves to Thy cause, let the vision of the ancient cross rise before us. Henceforth, let us truly live, move, and have our being in Thee. Lord, we are Thine. Use us according to Thy will. Amen.

SCRIPTURE: Acts 17:28.

* * *

O Thou, Lord of wonders and miracles which surpass all achievements and accomplishments of man, we praise Thy name. With humble hearts and contrite spirits do we confess our steadfast faith that Jesus, the Christ, is Thy only son, that he became obedient to death so that all sinners might be saved, and that he gained victory over death by his resurrection. He is indeed the savior of each one of us. Wilt Thou cleanse us of our faults and transgressions, and prepare us for the renewal of the new covenant. May this act of holy communion be acceptable in Thy sight, O Lord, our God and our redeemer. Amen.

* * *

Almighty God, who hast filled the heavens above with Thy glory, and the earth below with Thy love, we praise Thy name. We thank Thee for Thy beauty that our spiritual eyes behold, and for Thy voice that our discerning ears hear. Above all, do we thank Thee for Thy word that has become flesh and for our vision of his cross. Grant us faith and strength with which to exalt and magnify our blessed savior, as we humbly partake in this feast of the new covenant. Guide us, O Lord, through the path of peace. In Jesus' name. Amen.

*　　*　　*

Father of mankind, if ever our faith wavers, if ever our hope fails, and if ever our love wanes, let us reconsecrate ourselves at this feast. Wilt Thou nourish the best of men. Wilt Thou save the worst of men. May the towering cross stand forever, the eternal beacon lighting the way of life to the Christ. In his name we pray. Amen.

*　　*　　*

For the wonders of Thy creation, for the love of Thy Christ, and for the faith of Thy people, we thank Thee. As we partake of this feast of the new covenant, make us again prisoners of Thy cross. May the bonds of Christ's love eat into our flesh. May the chains of our faith bore into our souls. May we, within these bonds and chains, find eternal freedom and peace. In our savior's name, we pray. Amen.

* * *

Praised be Thou, O Lord, for Thou art omnipresent, omnipotent, and omniscient. We thank Thee for Thy word incarnate, even Jesus Christ. Bless this emblem which is about to nourish our faith in his victory over death. May this holy communion sustain us, though mountains fall upon us, though floods sweep over us, and though the forces of evil surround us. We pray in Jesus' name. Amen.

> NOTE: "Omnipresent" means present in all places, "omnipotent" all-powerful, and "omniscient" knowing everything.

* * *

Blessed be Thou, O Lord, for the crown of Thy creation, even Jesus Christ. With humble hearts and contrite spirits, do we commemorate his supreme sacrifice. May the vision of the ancient cross rise before us. May that vision remain in our hearts. May that vision nourish our faith. May that vision sustain our lives, though we walk in the shadow of death. Through Jesus Christ, our lord. Amen.

* * *

Our Father, Thou hast spoken, and the universe came to order. Thou hast spoken, and the Christ came to save. Thou hast spoken, and we come to participate in this sacred feast. May this precious emblem engender in our hearts the still small voice of courage, faith, hope, and love. In our savior's name. Amen.

* * *

O Lord, in whom we live, move, and have our being, we come to Thee trusting in Thy mercy unto us. As dew unto withered flower and rain unto parched land, so may this emblem revive our weary souls. As we rededicate ourselves to Thee at this Thy own table of the new covenant, may Thy watchful providence sustain us in the days to come. In comfort, may we not forget Thee. In suffering, let us remember Thy everlasting love. In Jesus' name we pray. Amen.

> NOTE: Generally speaking "new covenant" is understood to mean the New Testament, as in 2 Cor. 3:14 of the King James Version. The Hebrew word for "covenant" signifies agreement, rather than testifying.

*   *   *

O Thou, Lord, God of mercy and God of love, we thank Thee for Thy creative power of life and resurrection. In order that we may celebrate Christ's victory over death, humbly do we partake of this heavenly emblem. Cleanse us, remold us, and remake us according to Thy will, so that at last we may share in the glory of Thy only begotten son. In his name we pray. Amen.

*   *   *

O Thou, creator of the perfect image of man, we thank Thee for this feast of the new covenant. As we partake of this heavenly emblem, help us to face with grace all problems of life, to return good for evil, and to love those who hate us. Let Thy peace reign over us, like the silvery moon over the shepherd's tent. In our savior's name we pray. Amen.

NOTE: "New Testament" found in 2 Cor. 3:14 in the King James Version may be rendered new covenant.

* * *

Glory be to Thee, O God, omnipotent, omniscient, and omnipresent. We thank Thee for this precious table of the new covenant. With mercy look upon the observance of Thy own ordinance. With grace lead us to the ancient cross. As we partake of this blessed emblem, may bruised lives be healed, may crushed hearts be lifted, and may burdened souls be strengthened. In our savior's name. Amen.

NOTE: "New covenant" is referred to in Jer. 31:31 and in some texts of the Dead Sea Scrolls. To many Christians the Lord's Supper is an ordinance, rather than a sacrament. "Omnipotent" means all-powerful, "omniscient" knowing all things, and "omnipresent" present everywhere.

* * *

Our heavenly Father, we thank Thee for the revelation of Thy will in this precious ordinance. Though our earthly knowledge fails to comprehend the mystery of the manifestation of Thy love, by faith do we believe in Thy saving grace, and in trust do we partake of this emblem. Help us to enter truly into the fellowship of our Lord's suffering. Enable us to find therein that perfect peace which Thou alone canst give. In our savior's name we pray. Amen.

* * *

Blessed be Thou, O Lord, Father of mankind. From the earthly dust to the living soul, and from the living soul to the immortal life, Thou hast paved the way of the truth. In order that we may ever remember the priceless debt we owe to the Christ, do we humbly partake in this heavenly feast. Grant us, O God, adequate strength, saintly courage, and sufficient faith, which may ever kindle our hope for the true, beautiful, and good peace which Thou alone canst give. Amen.

SCRIPTURES: Gen. 2:7; John 14:27; Rom. 2:7; Phil. 4:7; 2 Tim. 1:10.

* * *

Wonderful Lord, precious Lord, we thank Thee for Thy only begotten son. In memory of his supreme sacrifice, do we humbly partake of this feast. Grant, O Lord, that our hands be empowered for the service of our fellow men and fellow women, that our shoulders be strengthened for sharing the burden of our neighbors, and that our faith be fortified for the edification of our friends. Let us find joy and peace in our wholehearted devotion to the cause for which Jesus died for us. In his name we pray. Amen.

* * *

O Thou, God of light, God of love, we thank Thee for this precious privilege to approach Thee in partaking of the feast of Thy own. Bless us according to Thy will. Cleanse us of our faults and trangressions. Enable us to envision, embrace, and enhance the power of the cross upon which Jesus died for us. In his name we pray. Amen.

* * *

Father of mankind, for the ever-present glow of our faith in the cross, we thank Thee. May it be with utmost humility that we partake of this heavenly feast. May it be with wholehearted devotion that we rededicate ourselves to Thy cause. May it be with complete confidence that we henceforth walk in Thy light. Through Jesus Christ we pray. Amen.

* * *

O Lord, our Lord, how excellent is Thy name. We thank Thee for the crown of Thy creation, even Jesus Christ. In memory of his precious life of sacrifice, do we partake of this blessed emblem. May the rock of Thy salvation withstand the dashing surge of human sorrows, disappointments and temptations. To the cross of Calvary be glory forever and ever. Amen.

* * *

For Thy many mercies and endless grace, do we lift up our hearts unto Thee in gratitude. As we partake of this emblem, may our conscience be reborn, may our lives be renewed, and may our homes be rebuilt upon the rock of Thy salvation. We abide in Thee, O great Spirit. Abide in us now and forevermore. Amen.

* * *

Our Father, we thank Thee for this feast of Thy heavenly love. As we participate in this holy ordinance, let us share the heavy burden Jesus once bore. Guide us along the shadowy path when we stagger. Show us the radiant cross when we are crushed. Lead us in the rocky path where the Christ trod. In his name we pray. Amen.

* * *

We thank Thee, O Lord, for this symbol of Thy redeeming love. With contrite spirits, do we partake of this ordinance. May the ancient cross sustain our faith. May that faith be the burning fire that consumes the power of evil. May that faith be the golden sunshine that yields joy to the world. May that faith be the silvery moonlight that gives us eternal peace. To the prince of that peace be glory and honor forever and ever. Amen.

* * *

We thank Thee, our heavenly Father, for Thy ever-unfailing love unto us. By virtue of that love, we approach Thee now in this sacred ordinance of our lord. By the new covenant in his blood, may we confirm our Christian faith. Through the cross of Calvary, may we rededicate ourselves to our master. Enable us at last to live, move, and have our being in him who is our savior and redeemer. Amen.

SCRIPTURE: Acts 17:28.

NOTE: Many Christians prefer "ordinance" to "sacrament." "Covenant" signifies a solemn agreement. "New covenant" refers to the Christian agreement with God through Jesus.

* * *

80

Our heavenly Father, we thank Thee for the power of Thy new covenant that has gathered us beneath one cross. As there is one Lord for all mankind, so may all peoples be one. As there is one table for Thy supper, so may all Christians be one. Let the principle of sacrifice be manifest throughout Thy creation. In Jesus' name we pray. Amen.

SCRIPTURE: Eph. 4:4-6.

NOTE: "Covenant" means agreement or solemn agreement with God. The Greek word for it is sometimes translated "testament" as in Mark 14:24 and 2 Cor. 3:6 of the King James Version. Many later English versions render it "covenant."

*   *   *

Most humbly do we approach Thee, our heavenly Father, as we participate in this sacred ordinance. We thank Thee for the cross. We acknowledge Thy love, and we believe in Thy only son. As he gave his precious life for us, so do we submit our lives to Thee, a living sacrifice. May they be acceptable to Thee for the upbuilding of Thy kingdom. In our savior's name we pray. Amen.

NOTE: "Ordinance" means authoritative command. It resulted, in this case, in the Lord's Supper. "The only begotten son" instead of "Thy only son" is also an acceptable translation.

*   *   *

Our redeemer liveth, O Lord. We thank Thee for his life, his death, and his resurrection. In memory of his precious sacrifice, do we partake of this divine feast. May the golden portals of eternal life be opened, and may we behold the jeweled crown of his everlasting glory. In Jesus' name we pray. Amen.

NOTE: Job 19:25 says: "For I know that my redeemer lives. . . ."

*   *   *

O Lord, let Christian zeal permeate our throbbing hearts, as we partake of this feast of the new covenant. May every drop of our sinful blood receive the redeeming blood of the Christ. May every morsel of our earthly flesh accept the heavenly flesh of our savior. May our whole person thus become a living example of the cross. Through Jesus Christ, our lord. Amen.

NOTE: "New covenant" means a Christian agreement with God. "Cross" in this prayer signifies the symbol of the crucifixion of Jesus, or the symbol of the Christian faith.

*   *   *

May Thy name be praised, O God of all mankind. We thank Thee for this our experience of Thy presence among us. May this experience remove all stains of our thoughts and render them as clean as the waters of the Jordan. May it erase all faults of our lives, and make them as pure as the snow upon Mount Hermon. May our self-dedication to Thy cause be acceptable in Thy sight, O Lord, our savior and our redeemer. In Christ's name. Amen.

> NOTE: The water of the Jordan is not always clean, but rather muddy during the rainy season, especially as it pours into the Salt Sea, commonly called the Dead Sea.

* * *

O Thou, master workman of the universe, in the crimson sky of the morn, in the violet heaven of the eventide, day after day, and night after night, the wonder of Thy wisdom surges within us. We thank Thee for this sacred emblem. As we partake in this holy feast, we pray that we might truly enter into the fellowship of the suffering of our blessed lord. To his eternal cross be glory forever and ever. Amen.

* * *

Glory be unto Thee, O Lord of hosts, for Thou hast given the Christ to all mankind. We thank Thee, O God of mercy, for Christ died for us. With humble hearts and contrite spirits do we partake of this blessed emblem. We pray that we feel within us the surging power of Thy redeeming love. Let it supplant fear with courage, doubt with trust, and disbelief with faith. Enable us to walk this day in Thy light. Through Jesus Christ, our lord. Amen.

> NOTE: The phrase "Lord of hosts" or "Jehovah of hosts" or "Yahweh of hosts" signifies God of army. Sometimes the hosts are identified with the children of Israel, as in Exod. 12:41. One primary meaning of the Hebrew word translated "host" in this phrase is service. So the children of Israel were to serve God, as soldiers do their commander.

*　　*　　*

We thank Thee, O Lord, for this wondrous table of Thy own appointment. As we partake of this heavenly emblem, let our eyes behold the risen Christ, let our ears hear his voice, let our mouths sing his praise, let our hearts rejoice in his promise, and let our minds rest in peace. Glory be to Thee, and to his cross, this day and forevermore. Amen.

*　　*　　*

O Lord, our Lord, how glorious and magnificent is Thy name, for Thou hast revealed Thyself in Christ Jesus and opened our vista unto eternal life. We thank Thee for Thy steadfast love which has brought us to this blessed table of the new covenant. As we partake of this heavenly emblem, help us to embrace the mystery of Christ's conquest over death. May Thy spirit enter our souls, and let us feel the beauty of Thy holiness. In our savior's name we pray. Amen.

> NOTE: "Steadfast love" in this prayer is the highest and noblest religious love, such as the love in Mic. 6:8, which is translated "mercy" or "kindness" in some English versions, and the love in 1 Cor. 13:13. There are several words for love in Hebrew and Greek.

*   *   *

Blessed Lord, Father of mankind, with humble hearts and contrite spirits do we speak unto Thee, trusting in Thy mercy unto us. We thank Thee for this table of the new covenant and for this emblem of Thy grace. As we partake of it, let us remember that our own lives were re-created in Thy image and likeness by the suffering of Thy own son. Henceforth, may our thoughts be pure, and may our words be righteous, and may our lives be blameless. Enable us to share the divine glory of Thy peace with all members of Thy household. In Jesus' name we pray. Amen.

> NOTE: "New covenant" means a new agreement with God, that is, Christian agreement compared to Jewish agreement, which is the old covenant.

*   *   *

O Thou, Lord of the universe and Father of mankind, we thank Thee for this holy emblem. As we partake of it, once again do we surrender ourselves to Thy care. As the suffering of the Christ forespoke his victory over death, and as the passing of the autumn bespeaks the coming of the spring, so may this renewal of the new covenant foreshadow for us thoughts that are clean, words that are pure, and lives that are perfect. Glory be to the crown of the Christ, now and forevermore. Amen.

> NOTE: "New covenant" here signifies a Christian agreement with God; that is, one's confession of faith in Jesus as the Messiah and one's commitment to his cause.

* * *

Glory be unto Thee, O Lord of the universe and Father of mankind. We thank Thee for this table of the new covenant. With grateful hearts and utmost humility do we partake of this emblem. Fortify us with Thy mighty word, purify us with Thy Holy Spirit, and sanctify us with Thy merciful command, to the end that each one of us may have a portion in the kingdom of heaven. Through Jesus Christ we pray. Amen.

> NOTE: For "new covenant" see the note to the preceding prayer. The liturgical reading of each section of the famous Talmudic ethical treatise, called Abot, begins with "All Israel has a portion in the world to come. . . ."

* * *

Our heavenly Father, Thou art omnipresent, omnipotent, and omniscient. We praise Thy name. We thank Thee for the benefaction of Thy grace, and for this table of the new covenant. As we partake of this blessed emblem, draw us ever closer unto Thee. May the shining star over Bethlehem rekindle our hearts, may the ancient cross upon Calvary enlighten our souls, and may we humbly follow in the steps of our master and savior. To this end grant us peace. For Thy name's sake we pray. Amen.

NOTE: "Name" in this prayer signifies person, as a personal name means a man or woman who bears it.

* * *

Our Father in heaven, in these moments of quietude bathed in the ray of Thy redeeming love, we thank Thee for this holy emblem. As we humbly partake of it, let it speak to us of Christ's victory over death. Enable us to offer to Thee our daily sacrifice of service to Thy cause. May the power of our faith dispel from within our hearts fears, doubts, desires, and wants, and fill our souls with courage, trust, devotion, and peace. Through Jesus Christ we pray. Amen.

* * *

Blessed are we, O Lord, for we are the disciples of the Christ. Blessed are we, O Lord, for we partake in this feast. Blessed are we, O Lord, for the Christ died for us. For these blessings we thank Thee. May Thy name be blessed, Thy son be blessed, and Thy church be blessed. For these blessings we pray through Jesus Christ, our lord. Amen.

NOTE: "Disciple" means learner or student. See Matt. 28:19, 20.

*   *   *

O God, for the perfect beauty of Thy creation, and especially for the mystery of Thy saving grace, we thank Thee. With grateful hearts and contrite spirits, do we renew our covenant in this sacred communion. We pray that, if the flower of our tree of life fades, let its fragrance linger for tomorrow; if its leaves fall, let them adorn the world to come; if its branches break, let them sustain Thy house of worship. Wilt Thou implant in our midst that tree of Christian faith and virtues. Through Jesus Christ, our lord. Amen.

*   *   *

Heavenly Father, we thank Thee for Thy word that has become flesh, for the burden of the cross which Thou hast placed upon us, and for this table of the new covenant. With humble hearts and contrite spirits, do we partake of this emblem. Hear us when we pray, teach us when we ask, guide us when we err, and sustain us when we fall. Lead us in the path of light and life toward the perfect image of the Christ. In his name we pray. Amen.

NOTE: "New covenant" is a solemn Christian agreement with God.

*   *   *

Blessed Lord, master of the universe and Father of mankind, we thank Thee for this table of the new covenant. In memory of the Christ's victory over death, do we humbly partake of this heavenly emblem. Though mountains fall, floods surround us, and burdens of life bear upon us, let us ever remember Thy saving grace. Enable us to embrace and embody that peace which Thou alone canst give. Through Jesus Christ, our lord. Amen.

SCRIPTURE: John 14:27.

NOTE: "Peace" in the Bible means not only the absence of war, but also sound health, perfect life, and general well-being. However, the Greek word translated "peace" in Mark 5:34, John 14:27, etc., signifies essentially the absence of strife.

*   *   *

Blessed be Thou, O Lord, king of the universe and Father of mankind. We thank Thee for this table of Thy saving grace and redeeming love. As we partake of this holy emblem, may the vision of the cross rise before us. Let it confirm, sustain, and strengthen our faith in Christ Jesus, and enable us to hear him say: "Your faith made you well. Go in peace." In his name we pray. Amen.

SCRIPTURE: Luke 7:36-50; 8:43-48.

NOTE: "Go in peace," which appears in these passages, is a very common greeting at parting even in modern Hebrew. However, it is appropriate here since "peace" means completeness or healthiness.

* * *

O Thou, Lord of eternity, may our prayers of adoration for Thy majesty over the universe, and thanksgiving for Thy love symbolized in this emblem be acceptable in Thy sight. As we humbly participate in this sacred feast, wilt Thou enter our hearts and let us think as Thou wouldst have us, and wilt Thou use our lips and let them speak Thy word. May our lives be truly cleansed, renewed, and refreshed, to the end that they may indeed reflect the beauty of Thy holiness. In our savior's name we pray. Amen.

Bread

Come Thou, almighty God. Look with grace upon these Thy children. Inspire them with Thy Holy Spirit, as they partake of this manna from heaven. May Thy light dawn upon their conscience. Let it kindle their faith in Thy promise. Let it give them rest in their mundane struggle. May peace reign over us, even as it does in heaven. Through Jesus Christ, our lord. Amen.

> NOTE: "Manna" is the name of the food miraculously given to the Israelites in the exodus. Exod. 16:31 says: "Then the house of Israel called its name 'man'. . . . " "Man" appears in the Greek and Latin translations of the Bible. "Manna" was probably taken from the Aramaic translation of "man." "Mundane" means worldly.

* * *

Our Father in heaven, hallowed be Thy name. We thank Thee for this institution of the new covenant and for this precious food from heaven. As we partake of this emblem, may the vision of the cross rise before us. Help us to realize that this act of our participation symbolizes the remission of our sins by Jesus Christ. Enable us to abide in Thee with clean hearts, steadfast faith, and eternal peace, both now and forevermore. In Jesus' name we pray. Amen.

> NOTE: "Hallowed" means made holy or sacred. "New covenant" signifies a Christian agreement with God.

* * *

We thank Thee, O God, for these golden moments of Christian worship. We now behold Thy glorious countenance. We now feel Thy unfailing love. We now live, move, and have our being in Thee. Facing the grim facts and dark realities of life, we now partake of this bread. Enable us to find faith in distress, hope in despair, and love in hatred. To the immortal cross be glory time beyond time and space beyond space. In our savior's name we pray. Amen.

* * *

Our Father, we thank Thee for this loaf. Wilt Thou sustain our faith as we partake of it. Enable us to gain that intelligent conviction which gives courage and hope, though we walk in the shadow of death. In Jesus' name we pray. Amen.

* * *

O Lord, like a torch in the dark the cross gleams in our hearts. As we partake of this precious loaf, may it truly feed our faith. Enable us to follow the gleam of Thy cross till the cycle of life marks its end. Through Jesus Christ, our lord. Amen.

*   *   *

O God, we thank Thee for Thy providence that has brought us together to this Thy own table. As we feed upon the bread from heaven, help us to reflect upon the true significance of this ordinance. May our burning passion for the cross and glowing faith in Thy word guide us in all relationships of man. In Jesus' name we pray. Amen.

> NOTE: "Providence" means benevolent guidance of God. "Ordinance" signifies authoritative command.

*   *   *

In the turmoil of human experiences, we now feel the tranquility of the radiant cross. We thank Thee for that cross that has conquered chaos and put the universe in order. As we commemorate that very cross which surpasses time and space, may we learn to nourish our souls with the bread from heaven. Enable us to feed upon faith, hope, and love. Through Jesus Christ, our lord. Amen.

SCRIPTURE: 1 Cor. 13:13.

*   *   *

Our heavenly Father, we thank Thee for this loaf, the symbol of our lord's broken body. We stand beneath the cross. We behold Thy son, even Thy only son. Help us to lay ourselves on that cross, and enable us to enter into the fellowship of his suffering. May we share that cross with our fellow men and fellow women. In our savior's name. Amen.

NOTE: The bread is regarded as an emblem or symbol among many Christians, but in some churches the bread is thought to be the body of the Christ.

*   *   *

We thank Thee for Jesus, for he shattered our bonds. We thank Thee for the cross, for it made us free. We thank Thee for this bread, for it renews our covenant. May we be ever grateful for Thy saving grace. Wilt Thou set our hearts aflame with zeal for the Christ. In his name we pray. Amen.

* * *

O Thou, Lord of light and Lord of love, we thank Thee for this blessed bread from heaven. As we partake of this feast of Thy grace, may the vision of the cross rise before us. Grant us the torch of Christian light. Guard us with the shield of Christian love. Enable us at last to share the burden of the cross. In our savior's name we pray. Amen.

* * *

We thank Thee, O God, for the rustling of leaves, the song of birds, the calmness of the starlit eve, and splendor of the sunlit dawn. With eager devotion do we partake of this bread. As Thou hast given us Thy only son, so may we learn to sacrifice ourselves for our neighbor. We dedicate ourselves to Thee, O God. Manifest Thy love through us in the turmoil of the human world, and the struggle of human life. In Jesus' name we pray. Amen.

> NOTE: The most common Hebrew word translated "neighbor" means friend or companion. The Greek word often so rendered signifies one who is near or close.

*   *   *

We thank Thee for this loaf. Humbly do we enter the golden portals of redeemed life. May the peace of the silvery moon be our guiding light, even as we walk in the shadow of death. In Jesus' name we pray. Amen.

> NOTE: "Shadow of death" reminds one of Ps. 23:4. Here, however, "valley of darkness" is preferred to ". . . valley of the shadow of death. . . ."

*   *   *

O Lord, humbly do we partake of this heavenly loaf. Wilt Thou cleanse us of our transgressions, and render our souls into the beauty and purity of snow. In our savior's name. Amen.

* * *

Our Father in heaven, quicken our humble hearts as we partake of this heavenly loaf. Enable us to enter into the mystery of Thy saving grace. In our savior's name. Amen.

* * *

Father, we thank Thee for the memories of the past, for the holy birth, for the wonderful ministry, and for the saving sacrifice of the Christ. May the star of Bethlehem illumine our hearts, as we partake of this loaf. In Jesus' name we pray. Amen.

* * *

We thank Thee, O Lord, for the dawn of conscience as we approach this table of Thy own appointment. Wilt Thou bless the loaf as we partake of it. Let the glorious rays of Thy unfailing love disperse the morning mist of our selfish pride. As Thou hast ordained the renewal of nature, so may we once again realize the debt we owe to the Christ. In his precious name we pray. Amen.

*   *   *

O God, creator of the universe, ruler of mankind, our Lord, and our Father, we thank Thee for Thy providence that has brought us nearer to Thee in this holy ordinance, and for Thy gift of the manna from heaven, which nourishes our souls by the grace of Jesus Christ. Let the vision of the ancient cross rise before us as we partake of this emblem, and let the voice of our blessed savior ring in our hearts: "Take, eat, this is my body, broken for you." Glory be to him now and evermore. Amen.

SCRIPTURE: 1 Cor. 11:24.

*   *   *

We thank Thee, O God, for the dawn of human conscience that is brought forth by the light of the new covenant. Realizing the debt we owe to our savior, do we humbly partake of this holy loaf. May our Christian faith guide us till the cycle of life marks its end. Through Jesus Christ we pray. Amen.

*   *   *

O Thou, Lord of the universe and Father of mankind, as we envision the ancient cross, how can we forget Thy saving grace? We thank Thee for this bread of life. With humble hearts and contrite spirits, do we partake of this emblem. Enable us to embrace the gleam of Thy everlasting love, and let Thy kingdom come to this world, in which Thou hast placed us. In Jesus' name we pray. Amen.

Wine

Father, we thank Thee for this fruit of the vine. As we partake of it, may we become worthy of the discipleship. Enable us to fulfill our Christian destiny with love and service, sharing the cross with the Christ. In his name we pray. Amen.

* * *

Lord, we thank Thee for this fruit of the vine. Humbly do we partake of this heavenly feast. Wilt Thou awake our souls from the scarlet couch of sin, and restore our hearts to the golden throne of the cross. In Jesus' name we pray. Amen.

> NOTE: Isa. 1:18 says: ". . . though your sins are like scarlet, they shall be as white as snow. . . ." Amos 6:4 says: "Woe to those who . . . stretch themselves upon their couches. . . ."

* * *

Our heavenly Father, we thank Thee for this cup. With contrite spirits do we behold the shining star of faith. May the truth of the ancient cross be our unfailing refuge, even as we stagger under the burden of life. Through Jesus Christ, our lord. Amen.

* * *

We thank Thee for this emblematic cup of Thy own ordinance. Help us to realize its significance and its meaning. Enter into our hearts and beautify our souls. Cleanse us of our sins and Christianize anew our lives. Teach us, guide us, and lead us for the sake of Christ, O God, our redeemer and our savior. In Jesus' name we pray. Amen.

> NOTE: Many Christians regard the Lord's Supper as an ordinance, rather than a sacrament.

*   *   *

Our heavenly Father, for the creativeness of man, which Thou hast bestowed upon us, we thank Thee. For our creative thinking we ask Thy guidance. For our creative being we ask Thy blessing. May our minds and bodies bear the mark of the cross. Help us to realize the significance of this cup. We ask this in Jesus' name. Amen.

*   *   *

Our heavenly Father, we thank Thee for this fruit of the vine, the emblem of the precious blood of the Christ shed for the remission of our sins. As we partake of this cup may we truly realize the debt we owe to him who became obedient unto death, that we might have abundant life. As we draw unto Thee in this sacred ordinance, enable us to walk humbly with our savior to the end that we may grow in his image. We ask this in his name. Amen.

> NOTE: Many Christians use grape juice as the emblem of the blood of the Christ. In some churches real wine has been served. For some Christian people the communion wine is thought to become the blood of Jesus.

*   *   *

In the quietude of this moment, we most humbly come unto Thee, our heavenly Father. Draw us closer to Thee now and evermore by virtue of Thy mercy unto us. Show us Thy countenance, O Lord, as we partake of this cup of the new covenant. Lead us into the gate of eternal truth, and give us the motive for the clean and wholesome life. In our savior's name we pray. Amen.

> NOTE: "New covenant" signifies the Christian agreement with God.

*   *   *

Our gracious Father, we thank Thee for Thy only son, the savior of mankind, in whose memory this feast is held. As we partake of this cup, may our souls follow in the footsteps of our lord, from the garden of Gethsemane to the cross of Calvary. Enable us to realize more fully the debt we owe to him for our redemption and to become more conscious of the meaning of the Christian life. Use us as Thou wilt, for the glory of him who died for us. In his name we pray. Amen.

> NOTE: The phrase "only begotten son," which appears in some older English versions of the Bible, is acceptable. But "only son" may convey the same meaning.

* * *

Our heavenly Father, we thank Thee for our Christian experiences and memories. In the bright sunshine, under the dark and cloudy sky, day unto day, and night unto night, the Christ is our strength and guide. As we partake of this wine, may we once again embrace his saving grace. Let it indeed sustain us now and during the rest of this week. In Jesus' name we pray. Amen.

* * *

We thank Thee, our heavenly Father, for this sacred ordinance of our lord's own appointing. In the quietude of meditation, we beseech Thee, O Lord. As we partake of this fruit of the vine, the emblem of our lord's shed blood, may our souls follow him from the garden of Gethsemane to the cross of Calvary, and may we thus enter into the fellowship of his suffering. Enable us to live, move, and have our being in Thee. We ask in Jesus' name. Amen.

> NOTE: "Ordinance" is an authoritative command. Many Christians regard the bread and the wine of the communion as emblems of the body and the blood of the Christ.

* * *

Lord, blessed Lord, there is none beside Thee. We thank Thee for this cup of Thy grace, reminding us of the remission of our sins and the conquest over death. Grant us the shield of faith. Give us the sword of the spirit. Let us follow the gleam of the cross now and evermore. Amen.

SCRIPTURE: Eph. 6:16, 17.

* * *

We thank Thee, our Father, for this blessed cup. With contrite spirits do we enter the golden portals of redeemed life. May the truth of the ancient cross be our strength, may the light of the beaming star be our guide, and may the peace of the silvery moon be our refuge, as we stagger under the burden of life. In Jesus' name we pray. Amen.

*　*　*

Father of mankind, we thank Thee for this feast of the new covenant. May this fruit of the vine symbolize the redeeming blood of the Christ. May this blood of the Christ signify his conquest over death. Enslave us, we pray, with the bejeweled chains of Thy love. Enable us, we ask, to bathe in the golden sunshine of Thy light. In Jesus' name. Amen.

> NOTE: The sacred communion is the feast of the new covenant, or the feast commemorating the Christian agreement with God. This involves one's confession of faith in the Christ and one's commitment to his cause.

*　*　*

O Lord, we thank Thee for this fruit of the vine. As we partake of it, may our souls embrace the zeal and ardor of fire. May Thy will be done. Through Jesus Christ, our lord. Amen.

> NOTE: The Hebrew word translated "soul" means person or individuality, whereas the Greek word for "soul" signifies breath as a sign of life. Other connotations of "soul" in the Bible are derived from these basic concepts.

*　　*　　*

Father, humbly do we partake of this blessed cup. Wilt Thou deliver us of our worldly bonds, and grant us faith in the unfailing grace and mercy of the Christ. In his name we pray. Amen.

*　　*　　*

Our Father, Father of all mankind, we thank Thee for this blessed symbol of redeemed life. As we partake of this cup, may our lord's crown of thorns become our crown of garlands, and may his burden of the cross become our burden of love. To that eternal faith be glory, forever and ever. Amen.

*　　*　　*

Father, open our spiritual eyes as we partake of this blessed cup. Help us to grow into the image and likeness of Thy son. In his name we pray. Amen.

* * *

Like a torch in the dark, the cross gleams in our hearts. Like a fountain in the desert, Jesus quenches thirsting souls. May this fruit of the vine feed our faith. Help us to follow the gleam of the cross. Enable us to drink at the fountain of life, lest we die, O Lord, lest our souls die. In our savior's name we pray. Amen.

NOTE: The "fountain of life" appears in such passages as Ps. 36:9 and Provs. 13:14; 14:27. "Souls" in this prayer signifies "persons."

* * *

O God, Thou hast brought forth the universe out of chaos and appointed man to rule over Thy creation. We praise Thy name. As we partake of this blessed cup, may we attain the mighty power of the cross. May we not be overcome by mundane disappointment and despair, but may we grow into the image of him who died for us. In his holy name we pray. Amen.

SCRIPTURES: Gen. 1:1-2:1; Ps. 33:6, 7; Isa. 45:7-13.

NOTE: According to the Hebrew text, Isa. 45:8-13 is a unit, and verse 7 concludes the preceding unit of thought.

* * *

We thank Thee, our Father, for the cross. As we partake of this cup, wilt Thou implant in our hearts the virtues of the cross. May it be our life's guide in all human associations, today, tomorrow, in the wake of birth, and in the shadow of death. In Jesus' name we pray. Amen.

* * *

O Lord, God of the universe and Father of mankind, we thank Thee for the Christ, the true incarnate of Thyself and the veritable flesh of Thy word. In token of our faith in his victory over death, do we partake of this fruit of the vine. May it become a seed planted in our soul, never dying and ever growing, until we may be led by Thy grace to the perfect peace, world without end. In his name. Amen.

> NOTE: "Incarnate" means that which has been made into flesh, and "veritable" true or real. "Peace" in the Bible signifies not only the cessation of war, but that which is sound or healthy, or that which is complete.

*   *   *

O Thou, rock of the transient world, we thank Thee for this cup of Thy grace. May our faith in the ancient cross purify every dimension of our feeling and willing. May it sanctify every sphere of our thought and action. May it magnify the Christ even unto the uttermost parts of Thy creation. We ask in his name. Amen.

> NOTE: "Transient" means passing quickly or temporary, and "sanctify" to make holy or purify.

*   *   *

Our Father, we thank Thee for this symbol of the grapes of Canaan. Awake our souls from the scarlet couch of transgressions. Restore our hearts to the golden throne of the cross. In our savior's name we pray. Amen.

> NOTE: "Canaan" is the area commonly known as Palestine. Today, it consists of the State of Israel, a portion on the west side of the Jordan which was a part of the Kingdom of Jordan, and the northern tip of the seacoast which belonged to Egypt. Canaan sometimes includes Lebanon and the Mediterranean coast of Syria also.

* * *

O Lord, more precious than gold is Thy son. More glorious than gems is Thy kingdom. More powerful than the sword is Thy word. We thank Thee for this fruit of the vine. Help us to conquer the whole creation with the light of the cross. In Jesus' name we pray. Amen.

> NOTE: In one of the Dead Sea Scrolls "the children of light" war against "the children of darkness," and in this war the former are triumphant over the latter. The contrast between light and darkness, good and evil, and spirit and flesh is familiar to the student of the Bible.

* * *

O Thou, creator of the universe, we thank Thee for Thy boundless love. Realizing our unworthiness, do we humbly partake of this wine. May the glory of the cross illumine burdened souls and darkened hearts, in the depths below without limit and in the heights above without end. We abide in Thee, O great Spirit. Abide in us forevermore. Amen.

NOTE: Wine, instead of water, was commonly drunk in Palestine, as it is today. Water is scarce, and it is not always safe to drink.

* * *

O Lord, we thank Thee for the saving power of the cross of Jesus. May our conscience be reborn, may our lives be renewed, and may our homes be rebuilt upon the rock of salvation, as we partake of this wine. In our savior's name we pray. Amen.

NOTE: Liquor consumption is not condemned in the Bible, but drunkenness is. However, the Aaronites were prohibited to drink when they went into the tent of meeting (Lev. 10:8, 9), and the Nazirites were not permitted to drink (Num. 6:2, 3).

* * *

O Lord, we thank Thee for the Christ, ever approachable, though never reachable. As we partake of this cup, wilt Thou draw us closer to that perfect person, even Thy only son. Once again do we dedicate ourselves to Thee. Wilt Thou strengthen our faith in the cross. In our savior's name. Amen.

*   *   *

O Lord, God of hosts and Father of mankind, we thank Thee for this heavenly feast of the new covenant. With utmost humility do we partake of this cup of Thy salvation. Enable us to drink from the fountain of eternal life. Help us to walk in the path of Thy divine light. Grant, O Lord, that we share the precious love of our blessed lord with all mankind. Glory be to the ancient cross, now and forevermore. Amen.

> NOTE: "New covenant" signifies the solemn Christian agreement with God, compared to the old agreement under Mosaic authority.

*   *   *

O Thou, merciful Father, we thank Thee for this blessed fruit of the vine. As we humbly partake of it, wilt Thou grant us courage when we are discouraged, strength when we are weak, Thy guiding light when we go astray, and Thy comforting spirit when we stagger under the burden of the cross. To that cross of Christ be glory forever and ever. Amen.

* * *

O Thou, gracious God and merciful Father, we thank Thee for this our faith in Thy revealed word, for this Thy table of the new covenant, and for this sacred emblem of the risen lord. As we feed upon this fruit of the vine, may we truly partake of the nature of the Christ. Re-create us and remold us according to Thy will, and let us live in peace for Thy sake. Through Jesus Christ, our lord. Amen.

> NOTE: "Revealed word" here means Jesus (John 1:14). "New covenant" is the Christian agreement with God, involving one's confession and commitment.

* * *

Blessed be Thou, O Lord, whose boundless mercy brought us here to this table of the new covenant. We thank Thee for this fruit of the vine. As we humbly partake of it, may the shining star of heaven enter our hearts, and may it illumine our pathway of life with the divine light above. Let our Christian faith and deeds blossom into the flower of eternal life. We ask through Jesus Christ, our lord. Amen.

> NOTE: "New covenant" is the solemn agreement with God, compared to the old agreement under Mosaic authority. The former is Christian, and the latter is Jewish, but they are closely related to each other. Early Christian people were Jewish, and they worshiped in the synagogue. The word "synagogue" is originally Greek, not Hebrew.

In the quest of the ultimate truth, we submit ourselves to Thee, O God, for Thou art the author of all, the creator of all, and Father of all mankind. May the threshold of this new year mark our steadfast advance toward Christian perfection. Let the bread of heaven strengthen our feet staggering under the heavy burden of the cross. In our savior's name we pray. Amen.

* * *

Our Father in heaven, we thank Thee for Thy providence which has brought us to these precious moments of communion with Thee. May the mystic power of this ordinance transmute the darker hours of yesteryear into the brighter days of the new year, and our earthly lives of yesteryear into the consecrated souls of the new year. Henceforth, let our renewed virtues guide us and our reawakened faith sustain us, as we press onward toward the perfect image of the Christ. In his name. Amen.

Palm Sunday

We thank Thee, O God, for the victorious entry of the Christ into Jerusalem, and for his ultimate conquest over death. Hosanna in the highest! May the recurring spring symbolize the cross of Calvary. May the bread of life emblematize the lamb of God. May the vision of the last supper rise before us as we partake of this feast. In Christ's name. Amen.

> SCRIPTURES: Matt. 21:9; 26:17-29; Mark 11:10; 14:12-25; John 1:29; 1 Cor. 11:23-26; Rev. 1:29.

> NOTE: "Hosanna" consists of two Hebrew words and probably means "Save, please!"

Easter

Praised be Thou, O Lord, for Thou hast created life, renewing itself in nature and man. We thank Thee for this renewal of the new covenant with Thee. As we humbly partake in this sacred rite, may we truly sense the emergence of new life out of our dying selves, and may this new life blossom into the glorious beauty of everlasting spring. Let our thoughts, words, and deeds embrace the purity of the Easter lily and the innocence of the risen Christ. In his name we pray. Amen.

> NOTE: "New covenant" is the Christian agreement with God, and "rite" is a solemn ceremony or observance.

116

Spring

O Thou, Lord of our destiny, we thank Thee for this table of Thy grace and for this emblem of Thy love. As we partake of this manna from heaven, may we truly renew our covenant with Thee. Henceforth, let us grow day by day into the image of the Christ, and let us blossom into the beauty of Thy holiness as Thy flowers of the spring. To this end, our Father, grant us Thy divine peace, as we share the burden of the cross. Through Jesus Christ, our lord. Amen.

> NOTE: "Manna" is the "bread from heaven." See Exod. 16:4, 15, 31, etc. The "divine peace" connotes much more than the cessation of war. It means completeness or perfectness.

*   *   *

O Lord, God of eternity, creator of the universe, and Father of mankind, we praise Thy name. We thank Thee for this sacred emblem of the imperishable body of the Christ. May it truly render us anew, so that we may worthily walk in Thy sight. Though the recurring beauty of the spring may perish, let us embrace the infinite beauty of Thy holiness. Though the mountains fall and seas rage, let Thy peace prevail over us, world without end. In our savior's name we pray. Amen.

> NOTE: The word "walk" in the Bible sometimes means to live, or manner of life.

*   *   *

Blessed be Thou, O Lord, for Thy creative wisdom and redeeming love. We thank Thee for this heavenly feast of the new covenant and for this divine symbol of our savior. As nature begins to wear the raiment of the spring, so clothe us with the garment of renewed life. As Thou hast enshrined in nature the power of revival, so instill within us the reborn faith in Christ Jesus. Let Thy word be fulfilled. Let the ancient cross illumine our hearts, this day and forevermore. Amen.

*   *   *

Blessed Father of all mankind, we thank Thee for the passion of Jesus Christ, whose shame and loss have released us from the bond of sin and death. May the mystery of this holy communion transmute our suffering to joy and transform our turmoil to peace. May the beauty of the spring tide embellish our souls with faith, hope, and love. In our savior's name. Amen.

Summer

Lord of the universe and Father of mankind, in the quietude of this summer morn and in the silence of reverent bliss, do we look up unto Thee and praise Thy name. We thank Thee for this sacred emblem. May we truly meet Thee afresh, as we participate in this holy communion. Henceforth, let us live anew for Thy sake. So strengthen us and guide us according to Thy will, to the end that our daily thoughts, words, and deeds will proclaim Thy saving grace. In Jesus' name we pray. Amen.

> NOTE: To many Christians, the bread and wine are the emblems, but other Christians believe that they actually become the body and blood of the Christ at the communion.

Autumn

Lord of the universe and savior of mankind, we thank Thee for the autumnal brocade without, the gleaming cross within, and this emblematic table before us. With grateful hearts and contrite spirits, do we partake of this fruit of the vine, and we pray that we may regain that purity of faith in trust like unto that of a babe on its mother's bosom. May the spiritual stars of Thy tender mercy illumine our pathway of life, though the day be dark, though the burden be grave. In Jesus' name. Amen.

*   *   *

We thank Thee, O precious Father, for the manifestation of Thy power of resurrection, which Thou hast enshrined in nature and man. In memory of the crown of Thy creation, even Thy own word incarnate, do we humbly partake of this sacred feast of the new covenant. Though flowers fade and leaves fall, let us recall Thy blessing of the summer fruits. When human strength wanes and earthly wisdom fails, let us remember the Christ's victory over death. Grant us peace, now and evermore. Amen.

> NOTE: "Incarnate" means made into flesh. Jesus is thought to be God's word in human form. During the summer months, it rarely rains in Palestine, but many fruits ripen then. See Jer. 40:10, 12.

*   *   *

O Lord, our God, and Father of mankind, we thank Thee for this feast of the new covenant and for our lord's victory over death. May this precious emblem instill within us a renewed faith in the ancient cross. When autumnal leaves fall, help us to remember the spring to come. When the day is dark, let us visualize the sun, the moon, and the stars of Thy creation. When we stagger under the burden of life, may we realize Thy sustaining hand of love. Through Jesus Christ, our lord, we pray. Amen.

*   *   *

Lord of the universe, God of mankind, our Father, we thank Thee for the precious sacrifice of Jesus Christ, for his priceless table of the new covenant, and for this life-giving emblem of Thy love. As we enter into the divine mystery of the Eucharist, let our souls die with the Christ, and let our souls rise with him. Weave us together in that harmonious beauty which manifests itself in the golden brocade of colorful autumnal leaves. Let us live for Thy sake. In our savior's name. Amen.

NOTE: "Eucharist" signifies thankfulness or gratitude. This is another designation of the Holy Communion.

* * *

Praised and exalted be Thy name, O God of the universe and Father of mankind. In the quietude of autumnal glory and in the beauty of Thy holiness, do we humbly bow before Thee, so that we may meet Thee afresh. Accept our thanksgiving, hear our supplications, and bless this table of Thine own appointment. Cleanse us, remold us, remake us, and use us according to Thy will. We rededicate ourselves to Thy cause. Have mercy upon us. Have mercy upon us. Amen.

Winter

Our Father, in these precious moments of quietude, do we look up unto Thee and praise Thy name. We thank Thee for this commemoration of Thy saving grace in Jesus Christ. May this act of our participation cleanse us and render us as white and pure as the snow that covers the handiwork of man this morning. Glory be to Thy handiwork, even the church of Christ. In our savior's name we pray. Amen.

*   *   *

We thank Thee, our heavenly Father, for this sacred loaf. As we partake of it, may our characters attain the beauty and purity of snow. May Thy kingdom come. Through Jesus Christ, our lord, we pray. Amen.

OFFERING

We thank Thee, our Father, for this opportunity to return to Thee a portion of that abundance that Thou hast given us. Cleanse it, and use it as Thou wilt for the glory of him who died for us. In his name we pray. Amen.

* * *

Father, we have dedicated ourselves to Thee. May this humble token of our devotion to Thy cause be acceptable in Thy sight. In Jesus' name. Amen.

* * *

As we have dedicated ourselves to Thee, our Father, so do we humbly express our gratitude in this thanksgiving. Consecrate this humble gift to the great cause for which the Christ died for us. In his name we pray. Amen.

* * *

As the Christ gave up himself that we may have eternal life, so do we humbly express our faith in this offering of thanksgiving. May it be acceptable unto Thee, O merciful God. We ask in Jesus' name. Amen.

* * *

O Thou, divine savior of mankind, the earth is Thine, and the fullness thereof. We and all that we possess are Thine. We thank Thee for this opportunity to share the fellowship of our lord's suffering and the joy of his resurrection. As we thank Thee for this communion of the saints, may this humble token of the re-dedication of ourselves and the offering of a portion of Thy abundant gift to us be acceptable in Thy sight. Glory be to the ancient cross, now and forevermore. Amen.

* * *

The earth is Thine, and the fullness thereof. We are Thine, and all that we possess. As we surrender to Thee a small portion of the abundance that Thou hast bestowed upon us, we pray that Thou wilt bless it, purify it, and use it for the glory of the Christ. In his name. Amen.

SCRIPTURES: Ps. 24:1; 1 Cor. 10:26.

NOTE: ". . . the fullness thereof" is found in the King James Version and in the American Revised Version. The Revised Standard Version renders likewise in Ps. 24:1, but in Ps. 50:12 this version has ". . . all that is in it" for exactly the same Hebrew expression. The New American Standard Version translates ". . . all it contains" in both passages. ". . . everything in it" or ". . . everything that is in it" in recent English versions is an indirect translation of the Greek text.

* * *

We thank Thee for Thy beloved son. Wilt Thou bless this portion of our rededication to him. To him be glory forever and ever. In his name. Amen.

*　　*　　*

Father we thank Thee for Thy saving grace and for Thy beloved son. Wilt Thou bless this humble portion of our rededication to his cause. Glory be unto Thee, now and forevermore. Amen.

*　　*　　*

We thank Thee, our heavenly Father, for this opportunity to glorify the Christ. Not that Thou seekest for our gifts, but that we may receive the spiritual benefit for Christ's sake, we bring these offerings unto Thee. Cleanse them and use them according to Thy will. In our savior's name we pray. Amen.

Winter

O Lord, may this small offering become a ray of sunshine and a drop of showers which usher in the Christian spring to this wintry and unbelieving world. In Christ's name we pray. Amen.

BENEDICTION

General

O Thou, guardian of our souls, teach us, guide us in our humble ministry, and may glory be to the ancient cross this day, and forevermore. Amen.

> NOTE: "Ministry" signifies service. It may not be limited to the function of professional ministers. Each Christian should be a minister of God, and of fellow men and women.

* * *

O Master, we are Thine. Enable us to abide in that steadfast peace, which surpasses human understanding and which Thou alone canst give. Through Jesus Christ we pray. Amen.

> NOTE: Biblical concept of peace is far more than Greek or Latin or English may imply. Its primary meaning in Hebrew is completeness; hence, healthiness or perfection.

* * *

May the lamp of Thy perfect wisdom illumine our minds, guard our course, and guide us to the higher destiny of Thy peace. Through Jesus Christ. Amen.

* * *

Now, O Lord, our faith looks up unto Thee, and we thank Thee for the Christ, our savior. Let us be drawn nearer unto Thee, and let us praise his name. Amen.

*   *   *

May God, the giver of peace, who brought back from the dead our lord Jesus, the great shepherd of the sheep, fit you by every blessing to do his will, and through him carry out in you what will please him. To him be glory forever and ever. Amen.

*   *   *

Lord, our Lord, let us truly minister to the Christ, and let his church become the fountain of Thy grace, mercy, and truth. Let Thy peace reign over us, world without end. In our savior's name we pray. Amen.

The Lord bless thee, and keep thee: The Lord make His face to shine upon thee, and be gracious unto thee: The Lord lift up His countenance upon thee, and give thee peace. Amen.

SCRIPTURE: Num. 6:24-26.

NOTE: This is called priestly benediction. One should be free to use "you" for "thee" and "to" for "unto," as do some recent English versions.

* * *

The grace of the lord Jesus Christ, and the love of God, and the communion of the Holy Ghost, be with you all. Amen.

SCRIPTURE: 2 Cor. 13:14.

NOTE: This is called apostolic benediction. One may use "fellowship" for "communion" and "Holy Spirit" for "Holy Ghost," as do some recent English versions.

* * *

Let the words of my mouth, and the meditation of my heart, be acceptable in Thy sight, O Lord, my strength, and my redeemer. Amen.

SCRIPTURE: Ps. 19:14.

NOTE: Here perhaps "my rock" is preferable to "my strength."

* * *

God be merciful unto us, and bless us; and cause His face to shine upon us, that Thy way may be known upon earth, Thy saving health among all nations. Amen.

SCRIPTURE: Ps. 67:1, 2.

NOTE: Here one may say "Thy salvation" or "Thy saving power" instead of "Thy saving health."

* * *

Now unto Him that is able to do exceeding abundantly above all that we ask or think, according to the power that worketh in us, unto Him be glory in the church by Christ Jesus throughout all ages, world without end. Amen.

SCRIPTURE: Eph. 3:20, 21.

NOTE: ". . . and in Christ Jesus. . . ." is perhaps better than ". . . by Christ Jesus." Familiar quotations are given here and elsewhere, even if they are not perfect translations.

* * *

The peace of God, which passeth all understanding, shall keep your hearts and minds in Christ Jesus. Amen.

SCRIPTURE: Phil. 4:7.

* * *

Now unto the King eternal, immortal, invisible, the only wise God, be honor and glory for ever and ever. Amen.

SCRIPTURE: 1 Tim. 1:17.

NOTE: "Wise" of "the only wise God" may be omitted, as in recent English versions. ". . . the King eternal" may be rightly rendered ". . . the King of ages" or ". . . the King of all worlds."

* * *

Now unto him that is able to guard you from stumbling, and to set you before the presence of his glory without blemish in exceeding joy, to the only God our savior, through Jesus Christ our lord, be glory, majesty, dominion and power, before all time, and now, and forevermore. Amen.

SCRIPTURE: Jude 24, 25.

NOTE: The word "authority" may be used instead of "power."

School

SCHOOL OF RELIGION

Convocation

O Thou, omnipotent Lord, omnipresent King, and omniscient Father. We praise Thy name as we approach Thy throne at the beginning of this school year. We thank Thee for these precious moments when we speak to Thee and hear Thy voice. We pray that we may discover that which our physical eyes do not see, that we may discern that which our earthly ears do not hear, and that we may experience that which our human senses do not comprehend. And in this holiness of Thy presence, let us yield ourselves to the cause of Christ. As we endeavor to partake of Thy wisdom in the days to come, let the virtues of love and humility bind us together in one spirit. Bless this institution of learning, especially its administration, faculty, and students, to this end. We ask in the name of Jesus, the Christ. Amen.

* * *

Mighty God, merciful Father, with awe do we stand in Thy presence, as we recall Thy mighty acts in history. With humility do we bow before Thee, as we remember Thy gracious words of salvation. With contrition do we surrender ourselves to Thy care, as we realize the seriousness of our ministry. May our academic endeavor during this school year lead us and guide us to that personification of perfect love, even Jesus Christ. Let us preach Thy word for its own glory and for Thy own sake. In Jesus' name. Amen.

*   *   *

O Lord, how excellent is Thy name. The cedars of Lebanon praise Thee. The roses of Sharon adore Thee. Thou hast given mankind the crown of Thy creation, even Jesus Christ. As we assemble here this morning initiating another season of our humble endeavor in this school of religion, we pray that in all that we think, speak, and do, Jesus Christ may be exalted. Be merciful unto us and bless this gathering to the end that we may truly sense Thy guiding hand upon us. In Jesus' name we pray. Amen.

Chapel

Father of steadfast love, accept our thanks as we bow before Thee at the beginning of this hour of meditation for all that which is good in our lives. Help us to realize that Thy constant care has brought us again to this period of prayer. May it be with rejoicing hearts that we approach Thee in prayer. Forgive our sins and help us not to do what is unnecessary, but to do what is important in Thy sight. May we examine ourselves once more in the light of Jesus' teachings and strive toward the higher goals of life. May we thus become better disciples of the Christ at the end of this service. In his name we pray. Amen.

> NOTE: "Steadfast love" is a more recent translation of the Hebrew word which was formerly rendered "lovingkindness" or "mercy." There are, of course, several other English words applicable for it, such as "kindness," "love," and "pious affection." For the repetitive usage of this word, see Ps. 136.

* * *

Mighty God and merciful Father, blessed be Thou, O Lord, for Thou hast brought us together to worship Thee. We pray that Thou wilt bless us according to Thy will, as we rededicate ourselves to Thy cause. Cleanse us, remold us, and re-create us, so that our ministry may become more acceptable in Thy sight. O Thou, great healer of the sick and wondrous comforter of those who are in despair and sorrow, especially those within our fellowship, be gracious unto them, and make them whole in body and in spirit. Now we ask that Thou wilt send Thy peace to all mankind, and let every person hear Thy gospel of salvation, for the world is Thine, through Jesus Christ. Glory be to his name now and evermore. Amen.

> NOTE: "Make whole" is essentially used in the Hebrew sense of peace, which means also health and completeness. See Matt. 9:21; Luke 8:48.

*　　*　　*

God of might, God of mercy, and God of wisdom, we thank Thee for Thy might that translates Thy will into action. We thank Thee for Thy mercy that makes saints out of sinners. We thank Thee for Thy wisdom that shows the way of the cross. Realizing our utter unworthiness for these wondrous gifts of Thy revelation, we recommit ourselves to Thee, and thank Thee for this opportunity to remind us of the precious mission of this Thy own institution of learning, its administrative officers, its faculty, its students, and its graduates. Be gracious unto us, and use us according to Thy will. Let us not be overcome by the wisdom of man, but let us overcome the world by Thy divine wisdom. Glory be to the ancient cross, now and forevermore. Amen.

*　　*　　*

O God who art the source of universal intelligence and cosmic energy, we praise Thy name. We thank Thee for the ordered knowledge of higher learning. May that knowledge, motivated by Thy will, manifest itself in all human relationships in such a way as may be acceptable in Thy sight. We now invoke Thy blessings upon this service. May we grasp its significance for Thy own sake and for the sake of human betterment. In our savior's name we pray. Amen.

> NOTE: "Knowledge" in the Bible has much to do with the knowledge of God based upon experience, such as meeting Him and talking with Him, rather than the ordered knowledge of man. This human knowledge should be controlled by God's will.

Dedication of Chapel Building

Mighty God and gracious Father, Thou hast delivered ancient Israel from the house of bondage. Thou hast revealed Thyself in Christ Jesus. Thou hast saved sinners from the destiny of death. We praise Thy name. Mercifully look upon this assembly, and bless the ministry of the saints who erected this Thy house of worship. From this day onward, let those who seek for Thy wisdom enter these portals, and let them go out as ministers of the new covenant. May this house of prayer truly become an instrument of the aspiration of the saints who envisioned the restoration of the church of Christ. Wilt Thou bless this gathering to this end, for we ask through Jesus Christ. Amen.

Faculty Meeting

Lord, our Lord and our Father, as we gather together to consider the matters which concern the education of ministers, we beseech Thee for Thy wisdom, knowledge and understanding. Forbid that we dwell upon our human desires and ambitions, but let us seek first Thy wisdom from above. We thank Thee for this privilege to participate in this gathering, and we pray that Thy guiding spirit rest upon us. May Thy will be done, O Lord. May Thy will be done here on earth. In our savior's name we pray. Amen.

Communion

Praised be Thou, O Lord, for Thou hast given us the breath of life and hast called us to the ministry of the Christ. Lest mankind should go astray in this transient world, Thou hast established the new covenant. We thank Thee for this Thy grace and for this Thy love. But, Lord, our sins are many, and our burden is grave. Cleanse us now with the dew from heaven, as we participate in this holy communion. May Thy presence and our fellowship be not mere symbols, but become a reality. May Thy word and our act be not mere rituals, but become life itself. Let this communion of the saints constrain us to serve Thee, world without end. In Jesus' name we pray. Amen.

* * *

Praised be Thou, O Lord, for Thou art indeed our maker, our redeemer, and our Father. Because of these relationships we gratefully acknowledge the debt we owe unto Thee. But, O Lord, while we declare our wholehearted devotion unto Thee, we sometimes wander about our selfish motives. While we preach Thy steadfast love unto us, we often become mindful of our selfish needs. So wilt Thou forgive our faults and transgressions, and cleanse us again for this renewal of the new covenant. Let us sincerely remember the advent, the sacrifice, and the resurrection of the Christ, as we participate in this sacred ordinance. May we truly become a part of that last supper which marked human history with Thy divine seal. Glory be to the Christ, world without end. In his name. Amen.

* * *

O Thou, Lord of the universe and Father of mankind, we thank Thee for this Eucharist, marking the end of another season of our humble academic endeavor. Let us be truly thankful for this apostolic feast of the new covenant, remembering Christ's own sacrifice for our sake, realizing his absolute lordship in our present lives, and reaffirming our total rededication to his cause for our future ministry. May this act of the holy communion with Thee and with our fellow Christian men and women render what is earthly to that which is heavenly, what is mortal to that which is immortal, what is perishable to that which is imperishable, and what is temporal to that which is eternal. Let Thy spirit descend upon us, and may this fellowship endure now and forevermore. Amen.

> NOTE: "Eucharist" means gratitude or thankfulness and signifies the Holy Communion.

Communion Benediction

Blessed be Thou, O Lord, we thank Thee for this Eucharist marking the commencement for those who have completed the primary disciplines of Christian ministry. May the imperishable body and blood of the Christ nourish the tree of these Christian lives dedicated to his cause, yielding abundant fruits for Thy harvest. Grant all of us renewed faith, hope, and love in Thy word incarnate, and may this Christian communion with our new graduates endure in Thy peace. Glory be to the ancient cross, now and evermore. Amen.

HONOR DAY

O Lord, how excellent is Thy name. From the temple schools of Babylonia to the court academies of Egypt, and from the forest colleges of India to the urban universities of America, the pearls of wisdom adorn the golden string of progress. But, O Lord, may it be from Zion that Thy wisdom whispers to our conscience. Let us bathe our intellect in the grace of Thy intellect. May Thy blessings rest upon this gathering and this institution of learning, as we honor the scholastic crown of glory, for we ask in our savior's name. Amen.

*   *   *

O Thou, Lord of the universe, Father of Thy own wisdom personified in Jesus Christ, and our Father, we thank Thee for this opportunity to honor those who achieved academic and religious excellence, and for this experience of our fellowship which has become a part of our lives on this day. May the galaxy of the stars of wisdom lead us to Thy perfect peace. For that peace we wait, for that peace we hope, and for that peace we pray. Glory be to the ancient cross now and evermore. Amen.

*   *   *

Blessed be Thou, O Lord, king of the universe and Father of mankind. As the sages of yore praised Thy name in China, in India, in Mesopotamia, and in Egypt, so do we adore Thee here and now for Thy gifts of intelligence, wisdom, and faith. Help us to remember that from ages past, where a temple stood, there existed a school also, and where worship was conducted, there underlay a means of instruction. We thank Thee for these new members of our honor society, who have demonstrated their intellectual ability, their ministerial zeal, and their fraternal good-will, and for others who are assembled here who aspire to these exalted objectives of the society. To the end that each of us may continue to endeavor to add another star of merit to the glittering chain of heavenly excellence which adorns the pathway of Thy servants, we pray for Thy divine light upon us. Indwell us, inspire us, and impel us, so that we may truly bear the torch of Thy love. In our savior's name we pray. Amen.

*   *   *

O Thou, Lord of wisdom, when Thou hast stationed the sun, the moon, and the stars in the sky to rule over Thy creation, wisdom was Thy master workman and was daily Thy delight. Blessed be Thy name. As Jesus was filled with wisdom as he grew and became strong, so may we attain, not so much the wisdom of the world, but Thy own wisdom through preaching Christ, the crucified. To this end do we humbly invoke Thy blessing upon us, especially upon those who join this day our distinguished honor society. May Thy guiding spirit rest upon them for the glory of the Christ, our savior. In his name we pray. Amen.

SCRIPTURES: Prov. 8:30; Luke 2:40.

* * *

O God, whether Thou art the personification of the best ideals of man, or the revealer of the truth and the savior of mankind, humbly do we acknowledge the inadequacy of human knowledge in the light of Thy wisdom. So we thank Thee for Thy providence which has brought us together, recognizing the academic excellence of the new members of this national scholastic honor society, and ask for Thy guiding spirit to rest upon them. To this end wilt Thou bless them, their teachers, and the administrative officers of this state institution of learning. May they effectively serve this community, this nation, and this world according to Thy will. Let us sense the manifestation of Thy abundant grace upon each one and upon this fellowship. Glory be to Thee, world without end. Amen.

NOTE: This prayer was offered at a state university.

* * *

Blessed be Thou, O Lord, Lord of wisdom, wisdom of the East, wisdom of the West, wisdom of the past, and wisdom of the present. We praise Thy name. Grant us, we pray, the guiding star of principle which may order human knowledge in harmony with Thy will. Through Jesus Christ, our lord. Amen.

> NOTE: "Wisdom" in the Bible is that skill which translates thought into action according to God's will. In the New Testament the Christ is identified with the wisdom of God. See 1 Cor. 1:24, 30; Col. 2:2, 3, etc. "Knowledge," in many passages in the Bible, is that understanding which is based upon experience.

Honor Day Communion Benediction

O Thou, Lord of light and author of wisdom, we thank Thee for this blessed fellowship which has ushered in the distinct communion of this honor society to this part of Thy creation. Henceforth, may Thy glory manifest itself evermore in our thoughts, our words, and our deeds, as we continue to minister to Thee and Thy children through Jesus Christ. Magnified and exalted be Thy name, O Lord. Let us go in peace. Through Jesus Christ we pray. Amen.

> *NOTE: "Go in peace," said Jesus to the woman whose faith in him healed her (Mark 5:34; Luke 8:48). This expression is still used in modern Hebrew. Though this Hebrew expression literally means "Go to peace," the Greek word for "in" in these New Testament passages could also mean "to" or "at."

BACCALAUREATE

Invocation

Blessed be Thou, O Lord. Thou hast brought us to the end of another academic year of our teaching ministry. As we recall the formative years of this Thy institution of learning, we cannot but sense Thy guiding hand over us. For this manifestation of Thy gracious spirit, we thank Thee. And now as we assemble here with steadfast faith and increasing hope for the church tomorow, may this become an occasion for rededicating ourselves to Thy cause. To this end sanctify us by Thy word, and grant us a portion in the community of the saints. Let us acclaim Thy son and proclaim his gospel from the dawn of the morn to the twilight of the eve of our lives. In our savior's name we pray. Amen.

Intercession

O Lord, exalted, extolled, and praised be Thy name, for Thou hast nurtured us in Thy wisdom and brought us to these moments of thanksgiving and rededication. As we seal our golden memories of this institution of learning in the treasury of life, may they motivate our continued endeavor toward a better ministry of Thy church. Wilt Thou dispel our complacency, and supplant it with the realization of our faults. Forbid that we should become boastful of ourselves, but let us glorify the Christ. Guard us against a self-centered ministry, but may our lives be Christ-centered, for we are Thine for his sake. In his name we pray. Amen.

* * *

145

O Thou, God of creation and Lord of salvation, humbly do we approach Thee upon this occasion, marking the end of another year of academic endeavor and the beginning of renewed dedication to Thy cause. May that which we have learned yesterday enrich our ministry tomorrow, and may that which Thou mayest reveal to us now affect our lives forever. So grant us, O Lord, that despite our faults and transgressions we become increasingly useful in the ministry of Jesus Christ. Let us lose ourselves for his sake, for he has given himself for our sake. Only thus let us live. Only thus let us serve. We are Thine, O Lord. Through Jesus Christ we pray. Amen.

* * *

O Thou, God of creation, Lord of salvation, and Father of mankind. Praised be Thy name. Thou hast shattered the Egyptian bondage of ancient Israel in Goshen, Thou hast released Thy exiled children from Babylon, and Thou hast given Thy son to the world that sinners may become saints. We thank Thee for this Thy ultimate revelation demonstrated by the self-sacrifice and resurrection of Jesus Christ. As we complete another season of our academic endeavor, humbly do we bring ourselves to Thee for fresh consecration to Thy cause and for sincere rededication of ourselves to Thy ministry. Wilt Thou open the doors of each day with the hand of merciful guidance, and close them each night with the hand of loving assurance. Grant, O Lord, that we receive Thy wisdom rather than human wisdom as we continue our studies, and let us never forget the time for thanksgiving for Thy grace abounding, and the time for repentance for our follies and faults aplenty; and let us be always willing to suffer for Christ's sake. May Thy truth prevail over us now and evermore. In Jesus' name we pray. Amen.

146

COMMENCEMENT

Magnified and sanctified be Thy name, O God, our heavenly Father. We praise Thy name, for with abundant mercy Thou hast nutured us, and with tender care Thou hast brought us to this day of commencement. May Thy guiding spirit rest upon this assembly, and may this become truly the day of our commencing wholehearted rededication to Thy cause. As we stand in Thy presence, enable us to realize that every moment and every place afford us the opportunity for Thy ministry, and every man and every woman present the need of Thy saving grace. And now may Thy divine spirit rekindle our flickering torch in the dark, and let it blaze its way to illumine every corner of Thy creation, to the end that all mankind may walk humbly in Thy light. To Jesus, the Christ, be glory forever and ever. Amen.

FOUNDERS' DAY

Blessed be Thou, O Lord, for the crown of Thy glory, for the scepter of Thy wisdom, and for the armor of our faith. We thank Thee for Thy gracious providence that has guided the growth of this institution of learning, for the prophetic vision of its founders, and for the words and deeds of its distinguished graduates. May Thy continued blessings rest upon the constituent divisions, colleges and schools, and may the woof of knowledge and skill now available in these academic halls and the warp of the ideas and ideals of the founders create an unending golden brocade for tomorow. Bless this gathering to this end, and to this end we pray. In our savior's name. Amen.

> NOTE: A university usually consists of colleges and schools. Generally speaking, colleges have undergraduate students, whereas schools have graduate students, in the United States of America. Divisions are sometimes sections of curricula and other times parts of the entire university organization.

ANNUAL CONFERENCE

Praised be Thou, O Lord, for Thou hast given us this blessed fellowship. We thank Thee for those dedicated Christian leaders who brought this institution of learning into existence and nurtured it to this moment. We thank Thee for these Christian heralds who are assembled here, so that they may actively participate in the growth of this school of the ministry, to the end that Thy gospel may be proclaimed throughout the world. We pray that Thy guiding spirit may rest upon each one of us, and that we may become better instruments of the Christ in illuminating this troubled world with the light of Thy word. In his name we pray. Amen.

ANNUAL BANQUET

O Lord, we thank Thee for the Christian memories and experiences that have been ours during the past year. We thank Thee, above all, for the intellectual gift that has been bestowed upon us, but wilt Thou forbid that we become too proud of it to be truly Christian. Help us to attain intelligent faith, hope, and love, but prohibit that we become too arrogant to become really Christlike. May we forever walk humbly with him who died for us. Bless this food and this fellowship to that end. In Jesus' name we pray. Amen.

149

ROTC COMMISSIONING CEREMONY

Praised, exalted, and extolled be Thy name, O God, creator of the universe and Father of mankind. We thank Thee for Thy providence that has nurtured this nation with Thy guiding spirit and tender care, for the heroes and heroines of the past who upheld the integrity of this government, and for the men and women of today and tomorrow who devote their lives to the safety of this republic and to the peace of the world. And now, O God, we invoke Thy blessing upon these cadets who are about to be commissioned here. Wilt Thou watch over them as they assume the duties and responsibilities placed in their hands, and may they in some measure enhance the ideals represented by the stars and the stripes of our flag. To this end we pray. Amen.

NOTE: Some cadets in this ceremony were Jewish; hence, the lack of Jesus Christ in this prayer. In any meeting of the church, however, there shall be no hesitancy in calling upon Jesus, regardless of the content of the audience.

INAUGURATION OF A PRESIDENT

Christian College

O God, the very foundation of the life of wisdom and the wisdom of life, we thank Thee for this opportunity to recall the past glory of this institution of higher learning, and to anticipate its future eminence, as Thou hast given us a new president. May his leadership signify the pivot of the vertical line of space and horizontal line of time, and may these lines spell the cross of the Christ. Wilt Thou bless him, guide him, and guard him to the end that all those who pass through the academic halls of this college bear the shield of faith, the helmet of salvation, and the sword of the spirit. Grant us all that wisdom beyond human wisdom, and that life beyond mundane life, O Lord, our God and our redeemer. Through Jesus Christ, our lord. Amen.

SCRIPTURE: Eph. 6:16, 17.

INAUGURATION OF FACULTY

School of Religion

O Lord, the glory of ancient Babylonia sleeps in the mounds of the Euphrates. The splendor of ancient Egypt rests in the ruins of the Nile. But it was the voice crying in the wilderness of Judea that heralded the majesty of Thy living word. May this faculty magnify the cross. May this institution exalt Thy kingdom. To the Christ, our king, be glory forever and ever. Amen.

SCRIPTURES: Isa. 40:3-5; Luke 3:4-6; John 1:1-5.

THANKSGIVING

America

O Thou, God of our fathers and Father of all mankind, we thank Thee for Thy providence that has placed us upon this galaxy of all galaxies, upon this planet of all planets, and in this nation of all nations on earth. We thank Thee for this beautiful America, with its purple mountains and amber waves of grain, with its spacious skies above and fertile soil below, and with liberty in life and justice in law. We thank Thee for our heroes of the past and heroines of yore, who founded this nation and nurtured its destiny, until now when fifty stars shine in one accord in our flag. As heirs of this precious heritage, we humbly pray for that wisdom and that faith which may enhance Thy name from glory to glory, world without end. Amen.

CHRISTMAS

Praised be Thou, O Lord, creator of the universe and Father of mankind. We thank Thee for the order which Thou hast ordained in nature, for the intelligence with which Thou hast endowed mankind, and for that word which Thou hast granted to the world. May the significance of that which is true, that which is good, and that which is beautiful prevail in our academic pursuits, and may we indeed become the bearers of the shining torch of brotherly love and eternal peace. To this end bless this gathering according to Thy will, for we ask in our savior's name. Amen.

> NOTE: "Christmas" is not found in the Bible, and not all Christians observe this feast on December 25. Some Christians do not celebrate this occasion.

EASTER

Praised be Thou, O Lord, for Thy creative wisdom that Thou hast enshrined in the universe. We thank Thee for the circuit of heavenly luminaries and the cycle of earthly seasons, which brought forth once again the song of birds and the smile of flowers. We pray that the academic urge of youth clad in the scholastic raiment of the spring grow into the maturity of ideas, ideals, and skills, which may be acceptable in Thy sight. May Thy intellect nurture our souls to the end that at last we may embrace the perfect image of the Christ. In his name we pray. Amen.

> NOTE: There is no Easter mentioned in the Bible, except in Acts 12:4, according to the King James Version. It should be Passover instead, as in other versions.

153

BENEDICTION

Mighty God, merciful Father, may the galaxy of stars of wisdom abide in Thy peace and perpetuate the generation of man. For Thy peace we hope. For Thy peace we wait. For Thy peace we pray. Amen.

> NOTE: God's peace includes much more than the cessation of war. It signifies rather the perfection of man by virtue of the divine grace. It is a result of man's wholehearted devotion to God.

* * *

O Thou, Lord of light and intelligence, enable us to shatter the bonds of ignorance and egotism, and let the shining torch of knowledge bring forth the surge of our zeal for the Christ. To his cross be glory, forever and ever. Amen.

* * *

May it be Thy will that mankind will embrace Thy wisdom and Thy peace. For this peace we pray. Amen.

> NOTE: God's wisdom far surpasses the wisdom of man, and His peace excels man-made peace. God's wisdom enables man to live according to His will, and His peace endows him with saintliness.

* * *

O Thou, Lord of light and wisdom, let the morning star of Thy intelligence guide the leaders of mankind. Let the evening star of Thy peace abide in the hearts of men. Let the sun and the moon of Thy order prevail throughout the world.

> NOTE: God's intelligence enables one to discern how to live according to His will, and God's peace grants one perfect satisfaction in life. This should be the ultimate purpose of education.

Miscellanea

GENERAL

May Thy name be praised. May Thy church be exalted. May Christ be glorified. Hear our prayers, O Lord. Amen.

NOTE: "Name" in this prayer signifies the person. It is the same as God Himself. In modern Hebrew "the Name" means God.

*   *   *

We thank Thee, O God, for the lamp of Thy word, for the light of Thy law, and for Thy path of eternal life. Guide us and lead us in that path of Christ. In his name we pray. Amen.

NOTE: The Hebrew word translated "law" means teaching or direction. It is related to an Akkadian word which means oracle.

*   *   *

O Thou, the light of the world, we praise Thy name. O Thou, the rock of salvation, we adore Thy name. O Thou, the Father of mankind, we glorify Thy name. Implant in our hearts the faith triumphant. Instill in our hearts the intelligence acute. In our savior's name we pray. Amen.

*   *   *

O Thou, rock of the transient world, we thank Thee for the light of thy word and the testimonies of the pious. Have mercy upon us, lest we should lose our footing. Let Thy countenance shine upon us, lest we should succumb to temptation. Teach us Thy statutes. Grant us good judgment. Guide us in the path of grace. Lead us at last to the fountain of living water. Amen.

SCRIPTURE: Ps. 119:129-136.

NOTE: "Rock" is used for God in several passages of the Bible such as Pss. 18:2; 31:3. "Transient" means passing quickly or fleeting.

*   *   *

We humbly approach Thee, O God, trusting in Thy mercy unto us. Help us to realize the limitations in human understanding, and so to maintain our faith at all times. May we not be troubled with the success of the unrighteous, but may we believe in Thy design of the universe. Enable us to cultivate our Christian courage, wisdom, and insight; and thus to follow in the footsteps of our master. In his name we pray. Amen.

SCRIPTURE: Job 12:2-12.

*   *   *

Our heavenly Father, Thou art mighty and merciful. With a profound sense of humility because of our unworthiness, we approach Thee. Wilt Thou show us Thy merciful countenance. Help us to be good members of society and faithful citizens of Thy kingdom. May we be prudent and listen to counsel. Enable us to be obedient to Thy word. Let the world understand Thee better through us, for we are Thine, forever and ever. Amen.

SCRIPTURE: Prov. 19:11-21.

* * *

Eternal Father, we praise Thy name, for Thou hast brought the universe from chaos into order, and from darkness unto light. Thou hast brought man from ignorance into intelligence, and from servitude into lordship. Help us to realize the mighty power of the cross. Enable us to appreciate the supreme sacrifice of Jesus. Implant in our hearts the law of faith. In our savior's name we pray. Amen.

* * *

Awaken our souls, O God, as we meditate upon these words. Jesus was and is the messiah from the beginning to the end. Enable us to realize the limitations of human understanding, but help us to believe in the extent of Thy authority. Vitalize ourselves with faith to be living witnesses in Thy kingdom. May we bear and share the cross even unto the uttermost parts of the world. In our savior's name. Amen.

SCRIPTURE: Acts 1:1-11.

NOTE: "Messiah" means one who has been anointed. Some kings, high priests, and other leaders were messiahs. However, to those who believe in Jesus, he is the messiah. *Christos,* from which the English word Christ is derived, is the Greek translation of Hebrew *mashiach*, namely, messiah.

*   *   *

O Lord, Father of mankind, Thou hast showed us the way of life through Jesus Christ. Implant in our hearts the Christian zeal for truth, honor, justice, purity, love, and grace. In Jesus' name we pray. Amen.

*   *   *

O God, the glow of the cross pierces through the darkness of human turmoil. Thou art our refuge. We trust Thee. Thou art our redeemer. We praise Thee. Thou art our shield. We fear not. Help us to speak Thy justice and righteousness. Enable us to gain Thy understanding and wisdom. May we abide in Thy law. In our master's name we pray. Amen.

Scripture: Ps. 37:30-40.

Note: "Justice" is the revealed will of God, and "righteousness" is that will practiced in life. "Law" signifies essentially God's teaching or directive.

*   *   *

O Lord, we come to Thee once again to reflect upon the essentials of life, and thank Thee for Thy simple gospel and the simple book. Help us to know the significance of Christian faith and experience in relation to the development of human society. May we not be haughty, but may we be humble in all relationships of man. Let us become truly disciples of the Christ. In his name we pray. Amen.

Scripture: Prov. 16:16-22.

Note: "Gospel" means good news. The act of God in the advent of the Christ is so marvelous and so profound that no human pen can fully describe it, but it is so simple that any adult can appreciate it. The gospel is much easier to understand, but far more difficult to practice than any philosophy or science.

ADORATION

O Thou, Lord of Lords, King of Kings, and shepherd of all shepherds, as we bow at Thy feet to thank Thee for Thy gracious care of the sheep, to confess our own faults and transgressions, and to plead for the fulfillment of our petition and entreaty, we cannot but glorify Thy name for the crown of Thy creation, even Jesus Christ. How marvelous Thy glory is, which manifests itself in nature! How wonderful Thy word is, which has become flesh in Christ! We praise Thee, we adore Thee, and we exalt Thee for the history of salvation from the exodus to the advent of the Christ, culminating in Thy gift of his church to all mankind. Blessed be Thy name, and blessed be the name of Christ. Blessed be his church. In his name we pray. Amen.

AMERICA

O God, in the crimson sky of the dawn and in the violet heaven of the eve, we humbly acknowledge the wonder of Thy handiwork. Thou hast indeed created the universe. There is none beside Thee. We thank Thee for America —beautiful not only in appearance but also in essence. May our love for Thee and for our neighbor dispel the human imperfections from this land and magnify Thy love throughout the world. May the stars and stripes of our flag abide in Thee, now and evermore. Amen.

> NOTE: God is the creator of the universe according to the Bible. The most difficult creation is that of order out of chaos, and the crown of God's creation is that of saint out of sinner.

BIBLE

O Lord, author of all, all-knowing, almighty, and ever present, we praise Thy name. We thank Thee for the book of all books, even the Bible, which Thou hast freely given to all mankind. Let it not remain a sealed book which the learned ignore and the unlearned shun, but let it ever be an open book to all seekers of the truth. May the heavenly wisdom of this book dispel the eloquent wisdom of man and restore our faith to the ancient cross of Jesus. In his name we pray. Amen.

SCRIPTURES: Isa. 29:9-14; 1 Cor. 1:19.

CHRISTIAN GROWTH

In the quietude of Thy glorious presence, we most humbly bow before Thee trusting in Thy mercy unto us. As learners of Thy holy word, we seek for Thy guidance in our pursuit of a better knowledge of Thy creation. As disciples of Thy only son, we seek for Thy benediction in our efforts in attaining true Christian character. As believers in Jesus, we seek for Thy blessings in our prayer for more profound and firmer faith. Wilt Thou grant us intelligence, character, and faith according to Thy will, for we are Thine to serve the Christ. In his precious name. Amen.

CHRISTMAS

O Lord, the voice of one that cried in the wilderness still resounds in our hearts. We thank Thee for the revelation of Thy will in Christ Jesus, Thy beloved son and exalted minister. We thank Thee for his love, so tender and so merciful that it shields even a bruised reed. We thank Thee for his word, so true and so righteous that it enlightens even a confused world. Help us to embrace a renewed faith in him, the faith which withstands even quaking earth and surging sea. In his name we pray. Amen.

SCRIPTURES: Isa. 40:3-5; 42:1-4; Luke 2:25-33; 3:3-6.

THE CROSS

Divine Father, for the cross of Jesus, we thank Thee. Through the cross of Jesus, we approach Thee. On the cross of Jesus, we rededicate ourselves to Thee. Enable us to bear that cross through joys and sufferings. To the lamb of God be glory forever and ever. Amen.

> NOTE: In several passages of the New Testament, Jesus is identified with the "lamb of God." See, for example, John 1:29 and Rev. 21:14, 22, 23. The Greek word for lamb in John and that in Revelation are not the same, but either may be so rendered. However, the "lambs" in John 21:15 is the translation of the Greek word found in Revelation.

* * *

164

Heavenly Father, let us flee for these few moments from the troubled world, so that we may again embrace the vision of the cross. We seek not the way of escape, but we do seek that faith and that courage with which to face the tasks and duties before us. Let us abide in Thee, O Lord. Abide in us, if it be Thy will. In our savior's name. Amen.

FAITH

O God, majestic, mighty, and merciful, humble words of man fail to describe Thee, but righteous hearts long for Thee. We drift in the turbulent current of this transient world. Help us, O God, to find the everlasting rock. Thou art the rock! By faith may we rest in Thy promise. By faith may we abide with Thy son. For we ask in his name. Amen.

> NOTE: God is sometimes called "my rock, and my fortress. . . ." See Pss. 18:2; 31:3; 71:3, etc. In the Hebrew language the root for the word "faith" and that for "amen" are the same. Its derivatives are translated "believe" and "be established" in Isa. 7:9.

*　　*　　*

O God, we thank Thee for the heroes and heroines of the past, who by virtue of their faith saw the unseen, heard the inaudible, and experienced the supernatural. Enable us to embrace that faith which perceives the ultimate cause of that which we see, hear, and sense. Help us to carry on by faith the Christian ideals and Christian tasks. Strengthen our conviction that in Christ Thy promise was fulfilled. By this faith may we resurrect into eternal life. This we pray in Jesus' name. Amen.

> NOTE: "Faith" in the Old Testament means essentially reliability or steadfastness, and "faith" in the New Testament belief or confidence; but both signify man's right relation with God. See Isa. 7:9, where "believe" and "be established" are derived from the root for "faith." See also Hab. 2:4; Rom. 4:5-22; Gal. 3:2-26; Heb. 11:1-40.

* * *

O Lord, from eternity unto eternity Thou art God. We thank Thee with confidence for the victory of our lord on the cross, and for Thy promise that those who believe may share in that glory. But we acknowledge our own human frailty and weakness, and pray that Thou mayest grant us that victorious faith in despair, distress, and disappointment. Through Jesus Christ, our lord. Amen.

> SCRIPTURES: Isa. 25:8; 1 Cor. 15:54-57; Heb. 12:1, 2; 1 John 5:4.

FREEDOM

Our heavenly Father, as Thou hast given freedom to the enslaved Israel, so hast Thou graciously set us free. As Thou hast effected release to the captive Israel, so hast Thou mercifully liberated us. As Thou hast rebuilt the ruined city of David, so hast Thou tenderly reconstructed our minds and our bodies. As we praise Thy name for all these, may we evermore realize our Christian duties and responsibilities as free men and women in Christ. Use us, we pray, Thy servants and Thy handmaids, according to Thy will for the glory of him who died for us. In his name we pray. Amen.

> SCRIPTURES: Exod. 13:3; Deut. 5:6; Ezra 1:5, 6; Jer. 30:18-22; John 8:32, 36; 1 Cor. 7:21, 24.

HUMAN ACHIEVEMENTS

Blessed be Thou, O Lord, creator of the universe and savior of mankind. Forgive us, O Lord, for we, mankind, usurped Thy government and Thy wisdom and have become proud of our own achievements. Forgive us, O Lord, for we, mankind, lost sight of Thy majesty and Thy love and have become worshipers of the golden calf. What we have made is hurting us. What we have produced is killing us. What we have invented is misleading us. We thank Thee for this challenge to stand by Thee and preach the gospel of the Christ in this mundane chaos. Let the voice of Thy church be as mighty as the roar of the lion of Judah, but let the ministry of Thy church be as delicate and tender as the lily of the valley. Let us not be hypocrites. Let us abide in Thee now and forevermore. Amen.

HUMILITY

Eternal God, love unexcelled, justice unsurpassed, and righteousness unequalled are Thine. Thou art indeed the Father of the Christ. May our pride in human wisdom, may the arrogance of human might, and may the complacency in human wealth vanish before Thee. Dispel the vanity before us and show us the light of Thy word. Grant us at last that exalted mission to preach Thy gospel to the world of mankind.

SCRIPTURES: Jer. 9:23, 24; 1 Cor. 9:15-18.

*   *   *

Our Father, we thank Thee for these few moments of meditation. Help us to examine ourselves anew. Forbid that we justify ourselves rather than Thee. Prohibit that we criticize others rather than ourselves. May we learn to respect anew those who have paved the Christian way of life for us. To Jesus who justified Thy love, who bore the cross, and who died for us, be glory forever and ever. In his name we pray. Amen.

SCRIPTURE: Job 32:1-22.

168

INTERNATIONAL BANQUET

Blessed be Thy name, O Lord, for the order of Thy creation that brought forth the nourishment before us. We thank Thee for the crown of Thy creation, even the creation of the children of man, to be partakers of Thy creative intellect. May the dream of the sages of the past become a reality in this assembly. May there be neither East nor West, neither North nor South, when strong men and women thus gather together. May Thy word lighten and brighten our path toward the realization of the unity of mankind, despite the diversity of cultures. Glory be to Thy golden throne, forever and ever. Amen.

> NOTE: This prayer was offered for an interfaith assembly; hence, the lack of Jesus Christ. Those who quote "Oh, East is East, and West is West, and never the Twain shall meet . . . ," from Rudyard Kipling's "Ballad of East and West," seldom recognize its latter half, which says, "But there is neither East nor West, Border, nor Breed, nor Birth, when two strong men stand face to face, though they come from the ends of the earth."

KNOWLEDGE

O Lord, the heavens declare Thy glory, and the firmament showeth Thy handiwork. With shame we submit ourselves to Thee for fresh consecration because, in spite of Thy merciful command, we have not actualized our duties to the full. Though not in a literal sense, wine and harp blind nominal Christian men and women. Wilt Thou dispel the cloud of our superficial customs and manners and enable us to gain insight of the true knowledge of Thee. Through Jesus Christ, our lord. Amen.

SCRIPTURES: Ps. 19:1-4; Isa. 5:11-17.

NOTE: For ". . . wine and harp . . ." above, see Isa. 5:11, 12. "Knowledge" in Isa. 5:13 means the knowledge of God. To know God means to become intimately familiar with Him.

*   *   *

O Thou, Lord of light and intelligence, enable us to shatter the bonds of ignorance and egotism. Grant us the shining torch of knowledge which may lead us to the renewed zeal for the Christ. To his cross be glory forever and ever. Amen.

NOTE: "Knowledge" in this prayer is the knowledge of God acquired through experience with Him.

LIGHT OF LIFE

O Thou, Lord of light, we praise Thy name, for Thou hast created light in the darkness of chaos and hast given mankind the light of life, even Jesus Christ. As we approach Thy throne of grace from the shadow of our mundane life, let the light of Thy word shine upon us. And as the Christ entered into the fullness of human life, so show us the way to enter into the fullness of his life. Bless each one who is in Thy presence, and let us feel Thy light penetrating our souls. In Jesus' name we pray. Amen.

MAN

Lord, blessed be Thy name. As we reflect upon the glory of Thy intelligence and power, we are but a particle of dust. Yet each particle Thou hast created, and each particle is a significant element of Thy universe. Thou hast made us of this particle, but ordained us only a little lower than Thee. Thou hast bestowed on us the crown of honor and granted us the dominion over Thy creation. We praise Thy name. Help us to attain and realize man's mission in this bewildered world. In Jesus' name we pray. Amen.

SCRIPTURES: Gen. 1:27, 28; 2:7; Ps. 8:5-8.

NOTE: The "angels" in Ps. 8:5 in some English versions is derived from the Greek and Latin translations of the Hebrew word which may be rendered "God" or "gods." Angels are occasionally referred to as "gods" in Hebrew, even though there is a definite word for them.

MISSION

O Thou, author of all, enable us to grasp the pivot of the cross, as the line of expanding human knowledge crosses the contracting line of the universe. Dwell within us as we bear the cross. May it purify every dimension of human thought and action. May it sanctify every sphere of human feeling and willing. Yea, may it glorify even the Christ unto the uttermost parts of Thy creation. In Jesus' name we pray. Amen.

PEACE

Praised be Thou, O Lord, for Thou hast given us the perfect gift of salvation. As we reflect upon our own anxiety and distress, we come to realize that we are weak within and we are imperfect without. Help us to communicate with Thee now and evermore, for Thou art our shield, our rock, and our refuge. Enable us to attain that peace which, transcending every human understanding, watches over us in Christ Jesus. In his name. Amen.

SCRIPTURE: Phil. 4:4-7.

NOTE: Peace is a significant doctrine in Judaism and Christianity, as in some other religions of the world. However, the peace in the Bible has the sense of completeness or perfection. When man's relation to God is perfect, there is peace; and this is the peace only God can give.

PRAYER

O Lord, I am undone. I do not know how to pray, for I cannot conceive of the inner cry of each person who has assembled here. But Thou knowest all. Hear us now and enable us to hear Thy voice. In Jesus' name we pray. Amen.

> NOTE: When one is asked to pray for others, one is often reminded of the response of Isaiah, "Woe is me! I am undone!" found in Isa. 6:5. Yet God knows the prayer of each person. Accordingly it suffices to ask Him to hear others' prayers, if it be His will.

* * *

Our Father, we do not know how to pray. Yet our inner souls cry unto Thee. Enable us to offer the kind of prayer that may sustain our sense of righteousness, the kind of prayer that may glorify Thee throughout the world, and the kind of prayer that may help us to abide in Thee at peace. We pray for truly Christian prayer, O God, through Jesus Christ, our lord. Amen.

> NOTE: Basically man can only pray that God's will be done. Man cannot believe that his will shall be done by prayer, unless it is God's will. If man's prayer controls God, that prayer leaves the realm of religion and enters the sphere of magic.

* * *

We thank Thee, O Lord, for these golden moments of Christian life, when we communicate with Thee. We now behold Thy glorious countenance. We now feel Thy unfailing love. We now live, and move, and have our being in Thee. Facing the grim facts and dark realities of life, we now meditate upon Thy word. Thou art indeed our rock, our refuge, and our redeemer, O Lord. To the immortal cross be glory time beyond time, space beyond space. Amen.

SCRIPTURE: Acts 17:28.

NOTE: It is entirely appropriate to say "in him we exist" instead of "In him . . . have our being" in Acts 17:28. More than fifty years ago James Moffatt rendered it ": . . it is in him that we . . . exist."

* * *

Our Father, dispel the veil of blindness of our own egotism, and let us behold Thy countenance. Disperse the clouds of deafness of our own conceit, and let us hear Thy voice. May Thy mercy sustain us as we endeavor to live according to Thy will. In our savior's name we pray. Amen.

RACE RELATIONS

We thank Thee, our Father, for Thy holy word that has become flesh in Jesus, the Christ. We thank Thee especially for the simple fact that there is neither color line nor national boundary in Thy kingdom. Enable us to supplant disbelief with faith, despair with hope, and hatred with love. May Christian grace, trust, appreciation, and goodwill be manifest in all social relationships throughout Thy creation. In our savior's name we pray. Amen.

SCRIPTURES: Mal. 2:10; Col. 3:11.

REDEDICATION

Glory be unto Thee, O Lord of the universe and Father of mankind, for Thou hast sent us the savior of mankind. As we rededicate ourselves to his cause, let Thy wisdom dispel the pride of human wisdom, let Thy might replace the vanity of human might, and let Thy riches supplant the boast of human wealth. May the ancient cross glow in our hearts from this moment on, even like the torch in the dark. Blessed be Thou, O Lord. Blessed be Thou, O Lord. Amen.

SCRIPTURE: Jer. 9:23, 24.

*   *   *

175

O God of Israel, God of the universe, and God of all mankind, great and merciful art Thou. Marvelous and wondrous are Thy gifts unto us. We thank Thee for Thy love that has been made real to us through the life of Jesus. May we live lives that are good, lives that are pure, and lives like the one of Jesus. Help us to examine ourselves and confess with shame that our lives have been far from the one exemplified by Jesus. May we consecrate ourselves anew and more fully, and give ourselves with wholehearted surrender to the task of upbuilding Thy kingdom. In our savior's name we pray. Amen.

NOTE: "Consecrate" means to make sacred, or set apart as holy.

* * *

O Thou, God of steadfast love, wilt Thou accept our thanks as we bow before Thee for the reality of Thy grace unto us. Give us the sense to trace that which is true, good, and beautiful in our lives unto Thee. Help us to examine ourselves before we judge others, and may we be generous with the faults of others and be kind to them. Let us be warned against failing to grow into the image and likeness of the Christ, and let us become more like him day by day. May we thus embrace Christian attitudes and practice Christian precepts in our social and religious lives. Glory be unto Thee and unto Thy son. We ask in his name. Amen.

* * *

O God, the only God, the eternal God, there is none beside Thee. Cleanse us of our transgressions, so that we may realize inward truth. Purify us of our iniquities, so that we may embrace clean hearts. Vitalize our faith and zeal for the cross, so that with renewed spirit we may restore the joy of Thy salvation. In Jesus' name we pray. Amen.

SCRIPTURE: Ps. 51:6-14.

*   *   *

We thank Thee, O God, for the burden Thou hast placed upon us. We looked for peace, but no good came, for we were not worthy of Thy cross. Help us to realize that our ultimate peace is the Christ. May the heavenly star of faith, hope, and love dispel the earthly chaos of distress, despair and hate. Wilt Thou accept our humble sacrifice, as we rededicate ourselves to Thee in one body through the blood of Thy son, in whose name we pray. Amen.

SCRIPTURES: Jer. 8:15, 18; Eph. 2:11-16.

*   *   *

O God, motivate in our hearts the urge for true worship. We thank Thee for Thy church, the body of Thy only son. Enable us to become more worthy of Thy call in his service. Instill within us the riches of this mystery, the Christ. May we find joy even in the ministry of suffering. For Christ's sake. Amen.

SCRIPTURE: Col. 1:24-29.

*   *   *

In these golden moments of quietude, humbly do we approach Thee trusting in Thy mercy unto us. As we rededicate ourselves to Thy cause, cleanse us, remold us, and remake us, according to Thy will for the glory of him who died for us. In his name we pray. Amen.

*   *   *

O Lord, our Lord, our wills are ours to make them Thine. Help us to make them so. Help us to make them Thine. Amen.

*   *   *

Our good Father, open our spiritual eyes as we bow before Thee, and let us behold the splendor of thy countenance. We thank Thee for the supreme privilege of ours to communicate with Thee, and we pray that our faults in the past for having neglected to talk with Thee may be pardoned. We thank Thee for the expansion of Thy kingdom and for the reality of Jesus. Help us to realize our responsibilities and duties as Christian men and women, and may we dedicate ourselves anew and more fully to the spread of the gospel of the Christ. In his name. Amen.

*　　*　　*

Amidst earthly turmoil and mundane chaos, Thy law sustaineth itself, fulfilled and graced by the Christ. We thank Thee for him, and we now commit ourselves to Thee, O God. Enable us to trust in him more earnestly. Help us to rejoice in him more faithfully. May we rest in him more peacefully. To Thee, the author of the supreme mind, be glory forever and ever. Amen.

SCRIPTURE:　Ps. 37:1-7.

NOTE:　"Mundane" means worldly, and "law" signifies teaching.

*　　*　　*

O Thou, master of justice, righteousness and steadfast love, we yield ourselves to Thee. Remold us, refashion us, re-create us according to Thy will. May this prayerful response to the challenge of Thy word be acceptable in Thy sight. Make us partakers of the burden of the cross. O Lord, our shield, our rock, and our redeemer. Amen.

*　*　*

O God, we thank Thee for the precious words of the wise. Wilt Thou remove the veil that covers the truth before us. Instill within us a spiritual balance for our words. Implant within us a qualitative scale for our expressions. Help us to know the vanity of many books. Enable us to break through the clouds of human superficialities, and let the beam of Thy divine love shine over Thy whole creation. For Jesus' sake, and in his name we pray. Amen.

SCRIPTURE: Eccles. 12:9-12.

NOTE: Usually Ecclesiastes is considered to be a book of pessimism. However, it speaks of the truth which we ourselves experience, and some positive instructions are not lacking. See, for example, Eccles. 12:1, 13.

*　*　*

Almighty God, from whom flows lovingkindness to the sons of man, we praise Thy name. We marvel at Thy creation. True are Thy words. We come to Thee once again to meditate upon them. Steadfast is Thy work. We come to Thee once again to ponder over it. Enable us to realize our weakness, nay, the weakness of all human power and intelligence, and to comprehend more fully the blessed new covenant in Jesus' blood. Thy counsel stands from eternity to eternity. And now we rededicate ourselves to Thee. May we bear the cross, world without end. In our savior's name we pray. Amen.

SCRIPTURE: Ps. 33.

NOTE: "Lovingkindness" or "steadfast love" appears in Ps. 33:5. It is rendered "goodness" in the King James Version. However, the Hebrew word means much more than any of these words. It has the sense of merciful and saintly piety. "New covenant" is the Christian agreement with God.

* * *

O God, Thy holiness transcends human emotion. Thy cross transcends human will. Thy son transcends human thought. We thank Thee for what we feel, for what we do, and for what we cogitate. We surrender to Thee, O God, our soul, our flesh, yea, our all. May unsurpassed glory crown the Christ, our king and our redeemer. In his name. Amen.

SOVEREIGN

Blessed art Thou, O Lord, king of the universe, who at Thy word bringest the twilight of the eve and dawn of the day, and who with Thy wisdom openest the gates of the heavens and the portals of faith. Thou are indeed the creator of the universe and the orderer of man's intelligence. We praise Thy name. Mayest Thou reign over us and over all mankind, for we ask in Jesus' name. Amen.

STATE LEGISLATURE

Blessed be Thou, O Lord, creator of the universe and Father of mankind. We thank Thee for our precious America, for our beloved state, and for its officers chosen by the people of this sovereign state. Grant that Thy law abide in these lawmakers. May Thy wisdom nurture their wisdom. Let the lamp of Thy word brighten their lamps. May Thy blessings rest upon this state government, in its legislative, executive, and judicial activities, that all may be for each, and each may be for all. May the golden star above the golden torch in the flag of this state shine forever, and may it contribute much to the perfect union of the stars of America. Amen.

NOTE: The flag of the state mentioned in this prayer is that of Indiana.

THANKSGIVING

For the serenity of Christian faith amid the turmoil of mundane chaos, we thank Thee. We thank Thee for the spiritual inheritance of this nation. We thank Thee for the historical heritage of Thy church. Above all, we thank Thee for that which makes us Christian. Help us to maintain our integrity, to trust in Thy promise, and to nourish clean thoughts, to the end that we may be thankful even in disappointment, distress, and despair. We thank Thee, O Lord, for Thy word which dispels the dark experiences of human life. For all of these, and for more, we thank Thee, in our savior's name. Amen.

SCRIPTURE: Ps. 26.

TREE OF LIFE

O God, the only God, the true God, our shield, our rock, and our refuge, we praise Thy name. Implant in our hearts the tree of the cross. May it be ever green and ever fruitful. Nourish the tree with Thy grace. May it be ever strong and ever prosperous. Help us to look up unto that tree in distress. Enable us to behold that tree in turmoil. Let it be our guide, our friend, and our all. In our savior's name we pray. Amen.

SCRIPTURES: Ps. 1:1-3; Jer. 17:7, 8.

NOTE: The tree of life in the Garden of Eden makes one think of the tree which is likened to the saintly man or woman. A Christian should be like the tree of the cross, for it is the source of eternal life.

TRUTH

O God, help us to think intelligently. We thank Thee for Thy word. We thank Thee for Thy creation. May we be intelligently religious. May we be intelligently moral. May we be intelligently intellectual. Above all, grant us the courage to abide by the truth. So let us act according to Thy will. Let us live according to Thy precepts. Let us serve according to Thy law. Glory be to the crown of the Christ, in whose name we pray. Amen.

SCRIPTURE: Ps. 15.

NOTE: This psalm contains eleven principles of practical life and is said to be a summary of all 613 laws of early Judaism. Note that these principles are teachings and not laws in the accepted sense of the word.

*   *   *

We thank Thee, O Lord, for our glorious consciousness of Thy presence in the temporal darkness of human turmoil. Towering above the mundane chaos of vanities and transgressions, let there arise within us Christian faith, hope and love. Help us to realize more fully that salvation is from Thee, not from man. Grant us that silent power of truth which has become manifest in Christ Jesus. In his name we pray. Amen.

SCRIPTURE: Ps. 62.

NOTE: The common Hebrew word for "truth" means reliability or dependability, whereas the Greek word for it connotes that which is real or actual. In the New Testament, however, the Greek word often signifies that which is sure or valid.

WISDOM

O God, let the firmament of heaven be shattered. Let the foundations of the earth burst. We cling to Thee, O rock of salvation, for we have dedicated ourselves to Thee, and we believe in Thy word. May our conduct be righteous and kind. May our speech be humble and gracious. May our thoughts be clear and clean. May we, above all, gain Christian wisdom. To the everlasting cross be glory, forever and ever. Amen.

SCRIPTURES: Provs. 4:7-9; 21:21-31; Eph. 3:7-13.

NOTE: "Wisdom" in the Bible is not the accumulated knowledge of books, but rather the ability to translate God's will into life. The Hebrew word for "wisdom" and the Greek word for it both have the sense of skill, even though this connotation is not always applicable.

*   *   *

Our Father in heaven, hallowed be Thy name. We thank Thee for Thy word that has become flesh. Help us to grow intelligent and wise in Thy sight. Forbid that we remain ignorant and foolish about Thy wisdom. Let it rule over us. Enable us to actualize thus Christian principles of life. In our savior's name. Amen.

SCRIPTURES: Prov. 16:22-33; John 1:14-18; James 3:13-18.

*   *   *

Our heavenly Father, we praise Thy name. Help us to gain the intelligence that pierces through the veil before the truth. Enable us to attain the virtue that breaks through the curtain before the righteousness. May we, above all, cultivate piety that will tear through the clouds before Thy countenance. Grant that we truly become Thy sons and daughters. Through Jesus Christ, our lord. Amen.

SCRIPTURE: Prov. 15:2-10.

NOTE: The contrast between the wise and the foolish is given in the above scripture. A wise man is a person who knows how to apply God's will to actual life. "Piety" in this prayer signifies religious devotion.

*　　*　　*

O God, the heavens declare Thy glory, and the firmament showeth Thy handiwork. We thank Thee for our urge for the good, the true, and the beautiful. Enable us to actualize this urge in sharing the fortunes and misfortunes of all mankind. Give us the intelligence to distinguish between the good and bad, between the true and false, and between the beautiful and ugly. May this intelligence guide us in attaining Christian grace and virtues. Let Thy glory manifest itself through us, if it be Thy will. Let us serve Thee for Christ's sake. Amen.

NOTE: The opening section of this prayer is taken from Ps. 19:1.

*　　*　　*

We thank Thee, our Father, for these words of Job. Thy wisdom transcends chemical formulas and physical equipment. Thy wisdom exceeds commercial appraisal and monetary price. Help us to understand that Thou alone knowest all, and without Thee wisdom does not exist. Enable us to comprehend that this wisdom is primarily religious and essentially moral. May the fear of the Lord, acknowledged through the Christ, cause us to depart from sins and transgressions to the end that the cross may be glorified. In our savior's name we pray. Amen.

SCRIPTURE: Job 28:12-28.

NOTE: In biblical Hebrew, there is no word for "religion." This concept is expressed by "the fear of the Lord" as in Job 28:28 and Prov. 1:7.

* * *

We thank Thee, O God, for that wisdom which transcends time and space. Help us to gain that wisdom which comprehends the creative order of the universe. Enable us to attain that wisdom which underlies the wondrous miracle of life. May our human knowledge accord itself with that wisdom which became flesh in Christ Jesus. In his name. Amen.

SCRIPTURE: Prov. 8:22-36.

NOTE: This is one of the most significant sections of Proverbs, in which God's wisdom is personified. It is something like the "word" in John 1:1-13, though they are not exactly alike. See also 1 Cor. 1:24, 30.

Appendix

"Pray constantly."—1 THESS. 5:17

Rut of Rote

God, save me from the rut of rote. A fixed routine of prayer is apt to become a meaningless act. Lord, I mean my daily prayers. Sometimes they aren't any good. Let me speak to you constantly, but each time afresh! Amen.

Forgetting to Thank God

Whoops, Lord, I forgot to thank you for your gracious response to my recent petition. Please pardon me for this negligence. Amen.

Two Hamburger Patties

How well I remember that day when we had only two patties of hamburger on our table, for we did not have the money to buy more. Our kids were hesitating to take one, and we did not intend to take any. And you remember, Lord, that I thanked you for that meat, because that was the most wonderful gift within that whole week, and you know that I have never been as thankful as I was then. Lord, let me learn to be more thankful for your gifts. Amen.

Human Ability to Think

I thank you, Lord, for your gift of thinking. I took a moment to think instead of acting like an animal, and you made me a better shepherd of your flock. Thank you again. Amen.

Prayer for Others

I am just thinking, Lord, that many of my private prayers are for my own benefit, and so few of them are for other people. On the other hand, so many of my public prayers are for other people, and so few of them are for my own benefit. Let me not be a hypocrite even in prayer. Lord, bless others more than you bless me. You are "my shepherd, I shall not want." Amen.

SCRIPTURE: Ps. 23:1.

Altruism

Ah, Lord, once again I was thinking of my own benefits when I should have been doing work for the betterment of others. Forgive me for my own selfishness. Amen.

Sufficiency

God, let me learn to say "Enough!" quickly, not "More, more, and more!" But let this be only for material greed. For spiritual growth, let me be a grabber of every opportunity for the Christ-ward advancement. Let me empty myself of earthly desires, so that the Holy Spirit may fill my soul. Amen.

Sanctification and Sacrifice

Lord, let me try to live my life cleanly and honestly. Let me endeavor to act justly and righteously. Let me learn to behave sincerely and lovingly. But, O Lord, I am asking all of these for myself. Am I selfish? Let me give my all to your cause. Lord, I mean it. Amen.

Righteous Minority

Thank you, Lord, for the courage you gave me to say, "No!" Why do some people seek after worldly recognition or mundane wealth? Why do they flatter and maneuver? I am confident that you will take care of me, if only I stay on your side, and I have never been disappointed. I thank you, my wonderful Lord. Amen.

Beautiful World

How beautiful the world would be, if only we did not have sins and transgressions! How beautiful mankind would be, if only we could find your breath in each man or woman! Why, even I am beautiful because you have created me. Let me keep and uphold that beautiful part—that part of the universe which belongs to you. Thank you, Lord, for beautiful Jesus! Amen.

SCRIPTURES: Gen. 1:26-31; 2:7; Ps. 8:5, 6.

Beautiful Face

Thank you, Lord, for the beautiful faces of the saints, not in shape or color, but the reflection of your holiness emanating from their countenances. A beautiful face belongs to every faithful Christian, a saint! Thank you for that beauty which we can find in any congregation throughout the world, if only we open our spiritual eyes to see. Amen.

Foolishness of Man

Father, where is the clean air which you gave mankind? Where is the pure water which you granted mankind? Where is the immaculate food which you bestowed upon mankind? Man is clever in his own eyes, and I admit that he has accomplished much for his own sake; but, Lord, he has contaminated his own environment, and now he is afraid to breathe, drink, or eat because he is wise in his own ways. Grant him your wisdom which has become flesh. Amen.

SCRIPTURES: Prov. 8:11; 1 Cor. 1:24.

Human Creation

Ah, Lord, saccharine, sodium nitrite, tris, laetrile, PCP, DBCP, asbestos, plutonium, and so many other creations of man overwhelm us. Will you please show our wise men and women how to use, and how to get rid of, what they have produced? Amen.

Three Minutes

Father, I have saved three minutes by using the best transportation, but I have wasted thirty minutes by looking at a meaningless TV program. I am sorry. Let me learn to use time wisely. Amen.

True, Good, and Beautiful

O God, let me fill my heart with what is true, good, and beautiful, and help me to dispel contrary thoughts. Amen.

A Bit More

Lord, let me learn to do always a bit more in my work than I am expected to do. I waste so much time, while utilizing modern equipment to save time. I say that I do not have the time, while spending much time looking at television. Let me not be a hypocrite. This I pray, O Lord. Amen.

Wife

One of the greatest gifts you gave me is my wife, for whom I thank you. Indeed, you have made her a "helper suitable to him." "A worthy wife, who can find? She is more worthy than any precious stones." I am ever thankful to you, O Lord. Amen.

SCRIPTURES: Gen. 2:18; Prov. 31:10.

Children

Our Father, you have given us our "image and likeness" in our children, and you have made us experience the meaning of parental love. What a wonderful love yours is, which caused you to give your own son to the world! Let us love you, as we ought. Amen.

Friends

Thank you, Lord, for my select friends, though I thank you for all of my friends. But I dearly appreciate friends like Job's who try to admonish me and teach me, even if they are a bit mistaken. I would rather have a few genuine friends than a multitude of social butterflies. Please let me be a select friend to some of my friends. Amen.

SCRIPTURES: Job 4:1f; 8:1f; 11:1f; 32:6f.

I Am Dying

Lord, I am dying, as is every man or woman. I began to die when I was born, and I am glad that I gave myself to you just in time, for ever since then I have been living in your peace. Thank you, Lord, for this living with you. Thank you, Lord, for this aging of my body, for with joy and trust I wait for the moment when my soul enters your kingdom. Amen.

Old Age

Why have so many and promising people passed away because of accidents or illness, and why do you keep an old man like me in safety and good health? You say it is not my business to ask such a question? Then if it is your will, please give at least a part of my safety and good health to more deserving young folk. You have been so good to me. Thank you, Lord. Amen.

Use of Money

Lord, how easy it is to raise and spend millions of dollars for pugilism, golf, football, and other athletic events! Now you know, Lord, that I am all for clean sports, but how difficult it is to raise and spend one million for the church! Will you please give the world a sense of values? Thank you, Lord. Amen.

Asleep on the Bible

What's the matter with me? I fell asleep while reading the Bible! It is a serious business to read your word of life. It should wake me up instead of putting me to sleep. Lord, what's the matter with me? You say, "Ask yourself." That's right. I am ashamed. I am awake now. Forgive me. Amen.

Tattooed Number

What a terrible feeling it was when I was seated next to that gracious Jewish scholar at the banquet! I saw on her arm the vivid number tattooed in the concentration camp in which she was once forced to live! My soul was crushed. Lord, I do not have the nerve to ask for pardon for that atrocity. Let it keep me humble all the days of my life. Amen.

Shattered Cross

Lord, the cross was shattered when the star of David was destroyed in the pogroms and in the Holocaust. Let us humbly acknowledge our brothers' inhuman guilt, regardless of our own faith and life. Glory be to the memory of those who perished for their faith in you! Amen.

> NOTE: Pogrom is an organized attack on, and massacre of, the Jews in Czarist Russia, and Holocaust here refers to similar acts of destruction of Jewish property and lives in Europe during the German occupation of the Hitler regime.